"As a doctor with 35 years of experience, [Simmons's] frontline experience with the challenges of maintaining life has given him insights that armchair and laboratory biologists never have."

—**Gerald Schroeder, PhD,** author of *The Science of God*
MIT-trained nuclear physicist and earth and planetary scientist

"Concise and well-stated...Read this book, whatever you might think. You'll finish it a different person than you were when you began it."

—**The *Statesman-Journal*,** Salem, Oregon

"I ended the book impressed that it takes quite a bit more faith to believe in evolution than it does to believe in a purposeful creator. But this book also explains the body's complex inner workings in a way that is easy to understand, and to remember."

—**Amy Givler, MD,** author of *Hope in the Face of Cancer*

"Sit back and enjoy as Dr. Simmons leads you on an exhilarating romp through your own anatomy...Explore the complexity of reproduction. Celebrate the miracle of your birthday. Examine the differences between man and ape. And in the end, be prepared to confront the overwhelming evidence against Darwin's explanation for your existence."

—**Dr. Jed Macosko,** molecular biologist
professor at the University of New Mexico

BILLIONS of
MISSING
LINKS

GEOFFREY
SIMMONS M.D.

HARVEST HOUSE PUBLISHERS

EUGENE, OREGON

Cover by Terry Dugan Design, Minneapolis, Minnesota

Back-cover author photo by Mikala A. Wood

BILLIONS OF MISSING LINKS
Copyright © 2007 by Geoffrey Simmons, M.D.
Published by Harvest House Publishers
Eugene, Oregon 97402
www.harvesthousepublishers.com

Library of Congress Cataloging-in-Publication Data
Simmons, Geoffrey S.
    Billions of missing links / Geoffrey Simmons.
       p. cm.
    Includes bibliographical references.
    ISBN-13: 978-0-7369-1746-9 (pbk.)
    ISBN-10: 0-7369-1746-2 (pbk.)
    1. Creationism. 2. Evolution. 3. Evolution—Religious aspects—Christianity. 4. Evolution
(Biology)—Religious aspects—Christianity. 5. Intelligent design (Teleology) 6. Darwin, Charles,
1809–1882. I. Title.
    BS652.S55 2007
    231.7'652—dc22
                                                                                    2006021722

Printed in the United States of America

07 08 09 10 11 12 13 14 15 / VP-SK / 10 9 8 7 6 5 4 3 2 1

Dedicated to my grandchildren—
Alex, Colton, Kyle, Ethan, Sam, and Sofie

"Human ingenuity may make various
inventions, but it will never devise any
inventions more beautiful, nor more simple,
nor more to the purpose than Nature does;
because in her inventions nothing is
wanting and nothing is superfluous."

LEONARDO DA VINCI

CONTENTS

ILLUSTRATIONS

FORETHOUGHT

"One cannot help but be in awe when one contemplates the mysteries of eternity, of life, of the marvelous structure of reality."

—ALBERT EINSTEIN

At a very precise moment nine months after conception, a hormone leaves the unborn child's brain. It travels across the placenta, enters the maternal circulation, and makes its way to the mother's pituitary gland. Although this hormone is a very complicated and convoluted chemical, its message is quite simple: *I'm ready, start the delivery process. My lungs have matured enough to breathe on their own, my heart is strong enough to assume control, my gastrointestinal tract is prepared to process food, and my brain is eager to start learning about the world. My ten trillion cells are poised to work together.* It's the unborn child, not the mother, who makes this decision. Then, the mother and child orchestrate the journey together.

This is not a spontaneous event. The mother's body began preparations the instant the sperm entered a selected egg. One might even argue that her body began preparing at puberty or even at the time of her birth. Her uterus, now enormously stretched to accommodate the growing fetus, is ready to squeeze down and push. The baby's head has been shifted downward with its arms at its sides and legs tucked in so that it can more easily pass through the birth canal. Only 3.5 percent of human babies present feet first or breech. The mother's breasts are engorged with food. Endorphins are flowing to help with the discomfort; hormones are giving her strong maternal instincts. Her vagina has secreted a special glycogen to prevent infection. A connection between the pelvic bones loosens to help the bony portion of the canal expand. Every maternal instinct has been primed. Every system is focused on success.

At first, the contractions come slowly, as if the uterus were warming up, but they quickly crescendo to more frequent and forceful squeezes. A myriad of different chemicals and hormones prompt and support every action as billions of muscle cells work in unison to break the bag of waters, dilate the opening in the cervix, and deliver the child.

■ ■ ■ ■ ■

This journey is often cited as the most dangerous moment in a person's life. Indeed it might be, yet every aspect of the process is well-coordinated, prearranged, rehearsed for millennia, and designed to bring a new life into being. Even the seams in the baby's skull bones have not yet fused, so that its unusually large head will be pliable enough to make it through. As the process unfolds, the adrenal glands add a blast of stress hormones to help the infant cope.

The newborn child will not breathe until it has cleared the birth canal. Anything sooner would lead to certain suffocation. It also will not wait too long. Rising carbon dioxide levels and falling oxygen concentrations will prompt that first breath. Otherwise, there could easily be permanent brain damage. The old slap on the behind belongs to the cinema. The inner workings of every newborn know precisely when to breathe, how deeply to breathe, and how to clear the debris inhaled from the amniotic sac.

Moments before mother and child completely disconnect, the newborn receives a last-minute blood transfusion from the umbilical cord. The placenta, which has been purposefully storing nutrients for this moment, infuses extra nourishment. And there is evidence that the fetus sends some of its own stem cells into the mother's bloodstream. These newly discovered *microchimera* stem cells seem to be purposefully left behind to help maintain the mother's good health. The child's survival might depend on it.

Every step is preprogrammed. Medical folks like to say they deliver a baby, but they mostly catch it. As the newborn takes its first breath, two tiny flaps inside its heart automatically close off a hole between the right side and left side of that organ, which then routes unoxygenated blood to the newly functioning lungs. A large blood vessel that connects the aorta to the lungs also automatically seals off. The artery in the umbilical cord shifts to servicing the new bladder. The placenta detaches on cue and follows the baby out. If it were to precede the child or detach prematurely, the consequences could be disastrous. Soon, the baby's remnant of the umbilical cord dries up and falls away. If any of these steps were to fail to occur or did not follow the right order, the human race would never have existed. They are a very complex, all-or-none phenomenon, an improbable collection of coincidences.

The baby arrives with a vernix coating to protect its skin. It also comes with a natural sucking reflex, and mother's first milk is purposefully loaded with all the right nutrients, minerals, vitamins, and a host of required antibodies. The newborn easily fits into the crook of its mother's arm, where the breast and nipple are strategically situated. It instinctively knows how to nurse—plus, it has a unique but temporary hump of high-caloric brown fat in its back, just in case. Lactation causes the secretion of natural contraceptive hormones that will suppress the mother's menstrual cycle. No need for a second baby to compete for mother's milk and threaten its survival.

■ ■ ■ ■ ■

This is the itinerary every one of us has to follow to travel here. Very specific and precise instructions have been passed down from generation to generation. The whole process is beyond complexity; it is an evolutionary impossibility.

If you steadfastly believe that these preprogrammed, constantly changing, and interdependent series of cellular events from conception to birth could have come about by trial and error, survival of the fittest, or a series of extremely lucky accidents of nature, there's no need for you to read on.

If you should read on, continue always to ask yourself what could possibly have been intermediary, successful steps (links) beforehand.

PART ONE
OVERWHELMING IMPROBABILITIES

1. HOW SCIENTIFIC IS THE METHOD?

Science and scientists should always seek out the truth no matter where it may lead. Scientific theories should always be open to intense scrutiny, repeated criticisms, and valid revisions, regardless of the source. Scientific thought should never assume the effect before proving the cause—or be a consequence of political correctness, religious fervor, or personal agendas. Students of science should always be ready to ask how, where, when, why, and sometimes who. And so it should be with every study on the origin of life.

Contrary to common belief, laboratory experiments have never scientifically proven Darwin's theory of evolution; nor have they proven Intelligent Design. It's very unlikely they ever will. Demands on supporters of Intelligent Design, however, to "scientifically" prove their position far exceed any demands placed on supporters of Darwin's theories. In fact, evolution scientists have been ignoring the tenets of their own scientific method:

Step 1. Observation

Step 2. Hypothesis formulation

Step 3. Prediction

Step 4. Testing of predictions

Most of academia insists that all experimental work follow these time-tested, time-honored, internationally-agreed-upon deductive rules to lessen mistakes and eliminate bias on the part of the experimenter. Many feel these rules should be the foundation of modern science. There are exceptions, of course—such as splitting a group of good-natured volunteers into sky jumpers with parachutes and sky jumpers without, to see which group sustains the worst injuries. Most exceptions, like this, are either too idiotic, too dangerous, or too obvious.

■ ■ ■ ■ ■

Darwin's theories should also be subject to the scientific method, yet there are no published experiments that clearly show one species naturally evolving into another species. Darwin essentially admits this in forgotten passages in many of his writings.

This is not about the faster rabbits escaping predators more easily or the breeding of different dogs into another shape, size, trait, quality, or look. Genetically speaking, a rabbit is still a rabbit, and the dog is still a dog. Survival of the fittest, on a short time line, is universally accepted. This is more about major transitions. No scientist has ever observed a natural collection of organic chemicals spontaneously linking up to form a protein, or thousands of different proteins, fats, sugars, and minerals combining to create a functional cell, or millions of different living cells fusing into a jellyfish, or a clam escaping its shell to become an octopus, or a fish evolving into anything remotely similar to an amphibian, or a frog transitioning into a lizard, or a bear developing a blowhole on the top of its head and an anus along its belly as it went for a millennium-long swim, or a monkey giving birth to anything humanoid. If Darwinian research cannot get past Step 1, then Step 4 can never be fulfilled. Even if fossils can be counted as Step 1, there are no proven transitional species—and therefore still no Step 4.

Beyond this, science often assumes our senses are truly reliable, our thought processes are completely trustworthy, our scientific measurements are entirely accurate, and most, if not all, physical constants have remained unchanged for millions, even billions, of years. Yet no one can truly know this.

There is little argument over the principles of natural selection, the premise of survival of the fittest (loosely defined), the categorizing of fossils, or the occurrences of mutations. These rules belong to both the theory of evolution and Intelligent Design, as do simple experiments—such as discovering how the barnacle's glue works underwater, how a kiwi bird makes an olfactory map, that a giraffe is born with protective hoof coverings, how an arctic tern can fly from the North Pole to the South Pole (and back again), that a breed of pink dolphins exists near Hong Kong, and how the Pompeii worm can survive scalding water.

TESTING AND PROOF

The scientific method requires the vigorous testing of any hypothesis. Since time machines have yet to be invented, scientists are left to their own imaginations and false realities. The infamous Urey–Miller experiment was one of these. A mixture of organic chemicals, presumably mimicking a primordial sea no one has ever seen, was subjected to electrical shocks. These "lightning strikes" produced a reddish, gooey tar that could not feed itself, defend itself, belch, hide, perspire—or mate with any other, heretofore-known gooey tar of the opposite sex. I would guess it was also hard to clean up.

One cannot prove Design, either. If you were to come upon an oil rig standing high above the water in the Gulf of Mexico, however, would you assume it happened by accident or by Intelligent Design? Design, of course—hands down. And so it goes with living beings, who are exponentially more complicated than all of the oil rigs in the world put together.

Professor William Dembski, nationally acclaimed author of *The Design Inference,* defines Intelligent Design as natural systems that cannot be explained in terms of undirected natural forces, yet exhibit features which, in any other circumstance, we would

---

A Key Option in All Investigations

Contrary to popular belief, *Intelligent Design is not merely a Judeo-Christian theory.* It belongs to every religion, every person, every living being. Also contrary to belief, it is not an alternative to "Science." Researchers still need to look under the hood. Students still need to know how a frog jumps, a bird nests, and a caterpillar changes into a butterfly. As Mark Cahill, author of *One Heartbeat Away* puts it, "You may find it hard to believe that God could make everything out of nothing, but the alternative is that nothing turned itself into everything." ID is an option that should always be discussed in the world of discovery.

---

attribute to intelligence. He points to the carved faces of four United States presidents—Washington, Jefferson, Lincoln, and Roosevelt—at Mount Rushmore. Given the natural forces of erosion, wind, and rain plus a rare push from a tectonic plate, it remains highly improbable, if not impossible, that Nature could have carved such likenesses.

One should apply similar logic to everything we see in Nature. This book will help explain why. When a species of animal or plant is too complicated to come about by chance, it must be caused by, created by, or guided by Intelligent Design (ID). One can argue, alternatively, that Design has occurred every moment since the "Beginning," or that the Designer merely made, and maybe revised, the rules.

In any case, modern scientists, despite public statements supporting newer Darwinian theories, are steadily disproving the theory of evolution. As they delve deeper into the chemical and biological sciences, the more complex and perplexing it is becoming. Ask any medical researcher how DNA, or more specifically our genes, came about, and you will more than likely get a shrug.

REQUIRED STEPS

The term *missing links* is often used rather loosely, but in order to scientifically judge Darwin's famous theory there needs to be further clarification of what qualifies as a link. These are mandatory, intermediate steps. They can be as small as an S-ring in a bacterial flagellum (tail) or one step in a long cascade of events to clot off a wound. Often, millions of steps—links—are needed to complete a process or move a species to a more complex level.

The Great Pyramid in Egypt is a good example of one step building onto another. Everyone agrees that this 450-meter-tall structure, the only surviving wonder of the ancient world, did not happen by accident. Two million limestone blocks ranging from 2.5 to 60 tons were mined and hauled from the Nile Valley. Construction could not have begun at the top and progressed downward or at the middle and outward. It followed a very elaborate architectural design. The newest level depended on the design, solidity, and security of the level or levels below. To be called a pyramid and function like a pyramid, construction needed to reach the peak. Notably, one cell of the human body is more complicated than this structure.

If, on the other hand, one expects written proof that a Designer did the designing, they will never see a Signature on the Job Order. If one wants to attend a lecture on "How I Did It," with the fanciest PowerPoint presentation ever, it isn't going to happen. If one wants an Invitation to observe the Watchmaker making his watches, it will never occur. Proof such as this will never happen.

An Inclusive Theory

Intelligent Design is not synonymous with Creationism. Every theory has different advocates, and those who believe in the literal interpretation of the book of Genesis are one of several supporting camps. Many ID proponents are not Christian; most believe the Earth is billions of years old; some believe dating methods remain flawed. This book is purposely written to argue on modern science's own playing field. Most, if not all, ID proponents believe that both the theory of evolution and religion's explanations are mostly faith issues. But there has been a very curious historical development. According to James Lovelock, author of *Gaia: A New Look at Life on Earth*, "Things have taken a strange turn in recent years; almost the full circle from Galileo's famous struggle with the theological establishment. It is the scientific establishment that now forbids heresy."

NO EXPLANATION

How complex is too complex for the theory of evolution to explain? The adult blue whale has 100 quadrillion cells, and each cell has up to one billion chemical compounds. How fast is too fast to be an accident? Enzymes work within cells at a millionth of a second. The impact of light on the retina to create vision takes 200 femtoseconds. A femtosecond is a millionth of a billionth of a second. When does a complicated life cycle speak against chance occurrence or a lucky series of mutations? There are known parasites that require at least two unrelated and distant hosts to complete one life cycle. There are insects that depend on protozoa in their stomach to survive, which in turn depend on even smaller microorganisms attached to them for survival. How impossible should a body part be? The lens of the human eye has 1000 layers of transparent, living cells.

Or, how unusual should a living species be before it defies the tenets of evolution? There are six-foot-tall gutless worms that live at the bottom of the ocean, plants that maintain internal temperatures higher than most mammals, carnivorous sponges, warm-blooded moths, frogs, and turtles that can survive being frozen, microorganisms that live on sulfur (not oxygen), fish that hibernate on land, a family of salamanders that can survive in a refrigerated jar of water for at least six years, fleas that jump 150 times their length 200 times a day, a breed of near-blind river dolphins who never sleep and whose eyes migrate upward after birth, a cuttlefish whose tentacles can shoot out at an acceleration of 25G after hypnotizing its prey, a tsetse fly that has only one offspring, and an illuminated deep-sea fish whose anus migrates from its left side to the rear.

Might each one of these be a collection of improbable coincidences?

Like many present-day species, the cuttlefish, whose tentacles can shoot at an acceleration of 25G and whose body can put on a hypnotizing light show to paralyze prey, has no clear-cut transitional ancestors.

© Georgette Douwma / Photo Researchers, Inc.[1]

All living beings, and millions of life-sustaining processes (eating, digesting, sleeping, drinking, healing, mating, reproducing, hunting…), must have had previous, simpler steps, all the way back to the beginning of life. This is not a linear chain, however, with a few missing links, like the drawing of a fish walking out of the sea and eventually becoming a man. Millions of genetic, chemical, and mechanical processes do not work in isolation; nor do they transition into new species in single isolated steps, as commonly found illustrations suggest. The overall picture evolutionary theory presents is more like a sky-high chain-link fence with more than a billion gaping holes. Or a trillion-dot Connect-the-Dots game with virtually all of the dots missing.

■ ■ ■ ■ ■

This book will show that the arguments supporting the theory of evolution are shaky at best, while nearly every aspect of science is compatible with ID. The fact that a frog can be dissected down to its minutest structure or thyroid hormone can be separated into amino acids in a research laboratory does not say science contradicts ID theory. The idea that a child will look like its parents easily supports ID-guided genetics or natural laws generated by ID. The fact that the strongest or fastest animals survive, the best camouflage works the best, the weakest die off, and mutations happen, is very compatible with Intelligent Design. Why wouldn't it be? The finding that a single fertilized egg the size of the period at the end of this sentence can develop into a seventy-trillion-cell being supports ID much more than it does Darwin's outdated theories.

Modern scientific studies have not made evolution more believable; they have made it less believable. There are exponentially more questions nowadays than answers. Scientific inroads into biochemistry, microbiology, immunology, ecology, parasitology, genetics, microscopy, and quantum mechanics (to name a few) have left the path of evolution littered with mud puddles, potholes, loose gravel, quicksand, detours, dangerous critters, and dead ends.

Based on the scientific method and the more than a billion missing links (and counting), one might argue that evolution no longer rises to the level of being a theory. Instead, it should be considered at most a hypothesis or, perhaps, just a proposal of historical importance.

2. IMPROBABLE COINCIDENCES

"I can see how it might be possible for a man to look down upon the earth and be an atheist, but I cannot conceive how he could look up into the Heaven and say there is no God."

—ABRAHAM LINCOLN

Most of us like to tell others about our personal coincidences, and we often believe that something mysterious and wonderful has happened. Whether these are purely statistical likelihoods or purposeful events, they often catch our attention. The more odd the coincidence, the more exciting the experience becomes. Many people can cite the day that they felt an irresistible urge to call home—feeling as if their child were badly hurt or a parent were in crisis—and promptly learned that not only was their premonition incredibly correct, but their timing precise. A few lucky transplant recipients have had their lives saved by coincidences. A few mountain climbers have safely fallen onto nearby ledges, and a few cars have hydroplaned into an empty lane. Those World Trade Center workers who were late to work on 9/11, I'm sure have been left to wonder.

There are numerous books written on coincidences, which is also called synchronicity. They typically include stories about long lost relatives finding each other or a wedding band found inside a trout 20 years after it fell overboard. One standout story tells about an unacquainted teenage boy and girl who were separated by a barbed-wire fence in a German concentration camp in the 1940s. Their only communication was a brief nod or slight smile from afar. Neither knew the other's name. Indeed, they knew nothing about each other. Forty years later, however, they ran into each other, somehow discovered the link, and soon married.

Another interesting story tells about male triplets who were adopted at birth by three separate and distant families. Years later, by mere happenstance, a college student began talking with another young man whom he presumed to be his best friend. This person, however, had no idea who the other was. After a few awkward moments, the uncanny error led to further introductions, where-upon the two look-alikes learned that they shared the same birthday, same birthmarks, and many of the same interests. A local newspaper carried a heartwarming story about adopted twins finding each other. The next day one of the boys received a phone call from another young man who was also identical in appearance, had the same birthday, and had the same interests.

We tend to celebrate our coincidences as being Providential and never notice the hundreds of opportunities that never happened. People who have had their cancers disappear with prayer think God intervened, but there are many others who have prayed and not been cured. The reasons for this remain unclear. Statisticians often say the chances of having a coincidence happen are relatively high given the billions of people on this planet. There's "nothing Providential about it," some have concluded. Also, our own personal thoughts, which may number in the thousands each day, are likely to coincide with something or someone that seems synchronous every once in a while.

■ ■ ■ ■ ■

So when does a coincidence leave the realm of a statistical prob-ability and step into the world of improbabilities? Can coincidences in compatible function, physiology, and anatomy happen in pairs, dozens, or by the hundreds in Nature? Can two fins just change because they want or need to into two legs with realigned bones, ligaments, tendons, nerve supply, muscles, circulation, skin, and purposes? In one step? In ten steps? Where are the eight intermediate steps? Can a whale dive to a thousand feet below the ocean's surface, pick a fight with a giant squid, and return safely to the surface without hundreds, if not thousands, of coincidental physiological changes occurring beforehand?

The bombardier beetle, for example, has many unexplained coincidences. This African insect can fire off two chemicals, hydrogen peroxide and hydroquinone, from separate storage tanks and rear jets. When the chemicals combine, they form a new chemical that burns the predator. The beetle can shoot these chemicals with an uncanny accuracy, as well, to either side, backward, or even forward, by swinging its tail under its abdomen. Special nozzles blast predators at a rate of 500 bursts per second, each at a speed of 65 feet per second. These chemicals are potent enough to severely damage a mouse and injure the eyes of any animal. In fact, human victims get a red eye called the "Nairobi eye." Yet these chemicals are entirely benign when stored separately at the back end of these beetles. How could this happen by accident? "Oops, those two chemicals didn't work" (spoken by an intermediate species). "Mind if I try two others before you eat me?" Or "Could you stand a little taller so I can get you with my nozzles?"

Keep in mind there are hundreds of thousands of chemicals on this planet to choose from. And even if the combo turned out perfectly right the first time, the beetles still needed a way to make them, store them, and fire them off.

The real links seem to be missing.

Joeys

A newborn kangaroo is an interesting combination of coincidences. A joey is born 33 days after conception. It is barely a half inch long and weighs less than a gram (that's smaller than a single peanut). Despite lacking functional eyes, ears, or hind legs, it immediately makes its way from its mother's womb across her lower abdomen and attaches itself onto a nipple located deep inside her pouch. This would be the equivalent of a newborn human baby crawling the length of a football field and finding its mother's breast in less than three minutes. Could an intermediate kangaroo predecessor have crawled halfway or survived without finding the nipple?

WHALES

The blue whale is the largest mammal on earth. The adult weighs up to 180 tons and reaches a length of 100 feet (roughly one third the length of a football field), yet the origin of all whales remains blurred. No one truly knows what animal or animals preceded them or how any of their unique capabilities came about.

Darwin once wrote that whales were the result of bears going out to sea with their mouths held wide open to catch insects, who, then needing to survive in the oceans, slowly changed—evolved—into these massive mammals. He was forced to retract that theory in subsequent editions of *The Origin of Species,* but this statement remains a typical example of his nineteenth-century thinking.

In olden days whales were only known to dive beneath the surface for variable lengths of time, breathe through blowholes, travel in herds, and be a good source of blubber. We have since learned that whales can dive many thousands of feet, make segmental, pressure changes at different parts of their bodies as they dive, withstand enormous temperature changes, communicate over thousands of miles, use their huge, triangular tail to accentuate propulsion downward, adjust *spermaceti* in their heads to regulate buoyancy, carry a large blood volume for extra oxygen, store additional oxygen in muscle tissues, carry nitrogen internally to prevent the bends, make use of flexible ribs to collapse their lungs at excessive pressures, maintain a filter in their bloodstream to keep gas bubbles from reaching their brain, shunt blood away from noncritical organs when oxygen concentration is low, vocalize without moving air, hunt by blowing a circular wall of bubbles to trap krill, and defecate from an anus in the lower front (rather than the bear's rear location). The deepest recorded dive of a sperm whale was 6560 feet, and the longest time underwater was 112 minutes, but unofficial records suggest they can go down 10,000 feet or more. Animals with a blowhole on top and the anus up front are not found in the fossil records.

Toothed whales use rapid clicks for echolocation, each lasting 1/1000th of a second. They emanate from the spermaceti organ, a mound on the forehead, named after its opaque fluid, which reminded Nantucket fishermen of semen. Many issue clicks at a frequency that is too high for us to hear, but some can deafen a person. This organ can also stun a passing fish for a quick meal. It lacks an evolutionary explanation.

THE GIRAFFE

The giraffe is another animal that lacks clear-cut predecessors. Its blood pressure of 280/180 and heart rate of 170 beats per minute are double a person's, yet it has a sponge-like organ at the base of the brain that absorbs all the extra blood that flows forward when the animal bends to drink. When satiated and the animal raises its head, it transfuses the brain so the animal will not pass out. That way it can deal with any pressing dangers and even take off running. According to Lynn Sheer, author of *Tall Blondes,* a plumber could not have designed it better.

Some theorists feel that the giraffe's long neck evolved to eat leaves that were higher up, but the late Professor Stephen Jay Gould of Harvard, who authored many scholarly pro-evolution books wrote that "this is a perfectly plausible idea for which there is no evidence." One would think that many species would have evolved a long neck through the same survival of the fittest mechanism. They have not. Also, younger giraffes eat from lower limbs. So what's the point of a long neck? Perhaps it's there to match the long legs, otherwise they couldn't reach to drink water. Why not have shorter legs so they can have shorter necks? Or, are those long necks actually weapons? The longer, the stronger? We know that male giraffes will battle for a female by slamming their necks together, and unfortunately, this can be a fatal encounter for one of them.

A six-foot-tall baby giraffe drops seven feet at birth, head first. They have softer horns that fold down as they pass through the birth canal and a gelatinous covering on their four hooves so they don't tear their mother's womb. They can walk within 30 minutes, run within an hour as fast as 52 mph, and nurse within two to four hours.

THE AMOEBA

The amoeba is a relatively large single-cell organism that can be found everywhere in the world. Although biologists have labeled its body parts and determined many of their functions, they are far from understanding the derivations and interactions. Although an amoeba's entire interior acts like it's all fluid, it can extend a false foot, called a *pseudopod*, forward while it simultaneously retracts the back end. That false foot can extend out from any spot along the cell surface, grow into variable sizes, and move in any direction—as if it can think, maybe even plan ahead. Decisions are being made with constantly changing, invisible scaffolding. Imagine a cube of Jell-O or a tablespoon of mayonnaise making purposeful moves around your dinner plate and eventually taking out a pea or a corn kernel.

An amoeba can pause, retreat, or attack. It can travel along a microscopic groove, escape a toxin or predator, hide in a micro-pit, or climb nano-stairs. Scientists are not entirely certain how it recognizes food and changes the pseudopod into a giant paw to engulf its prey. It digests its food with sophisticated enzymes, utilizes the nutritional components, and discards the waste. It is much more complex than any machine man has made yet.

There are no apparent predecessors known.

THE SCHISTOSOMES

Schistosomiasis is one of many diseases that totally defy the rules of evolution. It is caused by a parasite that affects 400 million people each year and kills about a million, yet there's a mandatory cycle that has to be followed or the organism perishes. Every step has to be done in a particular way, at a particular time, by a certain stage. Every step is highly complex.

The female schistosome produces hundreds of eggs within an infected human's bloodstream daily. These eggs know how to penetrate the walls of blood vessels, bowel, and bladder and then escape. This rite of passage can be devastating to the host. They travel in stool or urine into fresh water where they swell, burst, and swim away as a tiny larva called a *miracidium,* which is an entirely new form. This larva goes on a hunt for a specific freshwater snail and will track the snail's exhaust. Once inside the correct snail, this larva will produce hundreds of thousands of new larvae called *cercaria,* another new form. Most of these are released back into the water.

The cercaria are only 1/250th of an inch long, and they have only one day to survive. That means they must find a human host within 24 hours. They are equipped, however, and this is not a guessing game. They can detect minute amounts of fatty acids and waxes secreted by human hair shafts. The instant they catch the scent, they home in on the hair follicle, moving at incredible speed, dive into a microscopic abyss around the hair, and shed their tail as they penetrate the human host. This tail simultaneously emits a chemical attractant to other cercaria. "Hey guys, I found a human host," it basically says. Siblings follow suit, and soon both male and female worms, another set of new form, are traversing the person's bloodstream. They travel through the lungs and settle in the liver, where the blood is filled with fresh nutrients from the intestines. The larger male releases pheromones that attract a much more slender female. The two link up like a tiny green pea pod surrounding a skinny piece of dental floss. They attach to the blood vessels wall with suckers and produce a half trillion eggs in ten years, which slowly kill off their host.

How could this multistep process of entirely different forms and hosts happen by accident? Every step, every form, and every function of the schistosome's existence seems to be mandatory. There are many places along the way that this cycle could be halted such as urinating in a sanitation system or never going into fresh water, but given the status of most developing countries, that goal is hard to achieve. It only takes one person in the world to restart the entire cycle again.

MALARIA

Another intricate cycle and major worldwide killer is malaria.

An estimated 500 million people in developing nations are afflicted with this mosquito-borne disease and more than a million children die of it annually. The disease begins with fever and chills and not uncommonly progresses to anemia, seizures, coma, heart failure, and death.

This is a very specific life cycle that requires two hosts, the mosquito *Anopheles gambiae* (although 60 species can carry the disease) and a human being. An uninfected female mosquito bites and draws up blood from a person who is infected with malaria; there are millions of opportunities to do this in Africa, South America, and Asia. That blood meal will be loaded with male and female gametocytes that do not harm the mosquito. Instead, they fuse in the mosquito stomach into another form called *sporozoites,* who somehow know how to travel to the salivary glands of this insect.

Soon it's time for another meal, during which an uninfected victim is injected with highly infectious sporozoites that change to *merozoites.* The latter form will reproduce by the millions in the host's liver and red cells. New sporozoites are formed, another mosquito bites, takes on some infectious forms, and we're off to a new host and another cycle.

Recently, scientists have learned that people infected with malaria have a scent that attracts uninfected female mosquitoes. These insects can home in on any human being from dozens of yards away by merely recognizing the carbon dioxide we expel. It's sort of like bad garlic breath.

As with schistosomes this cycle will also not work unless all steps are in a row. Granted, there are many more opportunities, but this organism changes at least three times into a new form and lives within two specific hosts in different forms. How could this have happened by trial and error? Each host is a dead end unless a major change occurs.

HUMANS

In my previous book, *What Darwin Didn't Know,* I cover many of the missing links in the development of human beings. One link

▪▪ LIFE CYCLE OF THE MALARIA PARASITE ▪▪

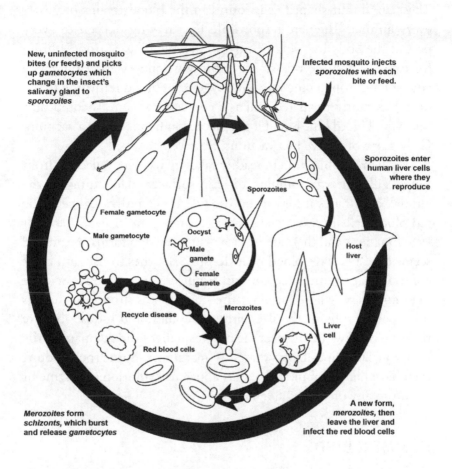

New, uninfected mosquito bites (or feeds) and picks up *gametocytes* which change in the insect's salivary gland to *sporozoites*

Infected mosquito injects *sporozoites* with each bite or feed.

Sporozoites enter human liver cells where they reproduce

Sporozoites

Female gametocyte

Male gametocyte

Oocyst

Male gamete

Female gamete

Host liver

Merozoites

Recycle disease

Liver cell

Red blood cells

Merozoites form *schizonts*, which burst and release *gametocytes*

A new form, *merozoites*, then leave the liver and infect the red blood cells

The disease of malaria requires two hosts, a mosquito and a human being, and it must go through multiple complex stages within each host. This entire cycle had to be in place as a whole from its beginning, or the organism would have died off long before the first cycle was completed.

Illustration by Dana Csakany.

not discussed, however, is the derivation of red blood cells, or rbcs. These are donut-shaped cells found in the bloodstreams of nearly every animal. They are responsible for carrying oxygen to every part of the body by using hemoglobin, which has a strong affinity for oxygen. You see this strong affinity whenever a person gets a cut—blood from a blue vein (unoxygenated blood returning to the lungs) instantly turns red when it contacts oxygen. Theoretically, one would bleed blue blood if the laceration happened in a vacuum. Only a few of us live in a vacuum, however.

The hemoglobin protein readily takes up oxygen molecules from lungs, gills, internal tubules, or skin surfaces, depending on the animal, and trades it for carbon dioxide at the individual cell. The red blood cells between species are not uniform in size, shape, or even functions and there are no clear-cut transition forms. An animal seems to either have blood or it doesn't. The rbcs in fish and birds are oval-shaped and they contain a nucleus. Ours don't. Science does not know where (or why) the nucleus was dropped. There is no apparent rule for rbc size, either. Elephant and mouse rbcs are the same size, while the deer's is much smaller. The salamander rbc is 100 to 200 times larger than any mammal's. Some species don't even have hemoglobin. There's no apparent evolutionary rhyme or reason to any of these differences.

HUMMINGBIRDS

These birds can only be found in the western hemisphere. They range from eight inches long in the Andes Mountains to bee-sized in Cuba; some can weigh as little as a penny. They can fly forward and backward, hover motionless, and even fly upside down; their wings can beat at an incredible 200 beats per second.

The hummingbird heart, when compared to its body size, is largest among warm-blooded animals. Its blood carries 50 percent more red cells per milliliter than a human, thereby maximizing oxygen-carrying capability. In the sports world this might be considered "doping." Its body temperature is considerably higher than ours during the day, averaging 105° F (but it can go to 110° F) to our mere 98.6° F; it can drop its temperature to 70° F at night, along with lowering its metabolism and heart rate. Birds that migrate can raise the fat content in their livers by 300 percent. According to Esther Quesada Tyrrell, author of *Hummingbirds: Their Life and Behavior*, a man would need a comparable 155,000 calories per day to match a hummingbird's metabolism, and his temperature might rise to 122° F.

The muscle structure of hummingbirds is quite different than other birds. The chest muscles, for one, are a much larger percentage, and their cells contain giant mitochondria. These are the power generators found in every living cell. The hummingbird breathes at a rate of 250 times or more per minute, whereas many birds breathe at under 30 times a minute. When overheated, this bird pants. It also has eight pair of ribs when most birds have six pairs.

The hummingbird has a long, forked, translucent tongue that has special musculature that can extend it deep inside flowers. It does not suck, however, but licks nectar at a rate of 13 times a second.

There are no clear-cut predecessors.

OTHERS

The illuminated netdevil is a fish that lives at a depth of three-and-a-half kilometers (over two miles) in the ocean. It has brightly lit branching appendages that have led some to calling it an oceangoing Christmas tree. It also has an unprecedented quirk of its anatomy. Its anus opens along the left side of its body while it's young and then it migrates to midline later in life. The male netdevil, which is much smaller than the female, attaches to her side and lives off of her blood.

Another unexplained anatomy quirk is the migrating eye of a flounder. These are bottom fish who swim upright and have eyes on both sides like any fish. Later, when they bury themselves in the sand, the downside eye migrates around so that they will have binocular vision.

The Komodo dragon from the island of Komodo in Indonesia can reach a length of 15 feet and stand 3 feet high. Its family, called *varanids,* are the only reptiles that chew their food with teeth. Turtles "cut up their prey"—use scales at the entrance to their mouth—and all other reptiles do a tear-and-gulp number. The Komodo dragon is a scavenger that is known for having the worst breath on the planet. It prefers its food dead for a few days (and not refrigerated), but it will also charge a deer, goat, cow, and even a human. Its mouth carries a particularly virulent bacteria, which it injects with a deep bite. It then stalks the victim by the smell of infected flesh. When the animal is weakened, it will move in for the kill. It will swallow horns, bones, and skull entirely with different chomps. It also has a third eye on top of its head, probably to regulate activity based on availability of sunlight.

Certain microbes in the ocean feed on other microbes that possess chloroplasts, which are microscopic organelles that make food by photosynthesis. Before they devour them, they suck out the chloroplasts and enslave them for their own internal food manufacturing. The much larger sea slug *elysia* grazes on seaweed called dead-man's fingers. Instead of eating the lobes, however, it sucks out the chloroplasts and also uses them to make food.

Every year in May during a full moon and high tide for 300 million years, hundreds of thousands of horseshoe crabs come ashore in Delaware Bay to breed. In fact, nothing has changed for 300 million years in these gentle creatures, which are related more to scorpions than crabs. They have multiple, specialized legs and nine eyes. They can swim upside down with flapping gills; they are well designed to flip over if stuck on their back and to dig in the sand. They may be the oldest living species—and not one of them, as best as we can tell, has changed to walking erect, reciting poetry, or sending spacecraft to Pluto.

No obvious predecessors known.

■ ■ ■ ■ ■

When one looks closely at visual functions, the number of

missing links is figuratively blinding. Presumably, the ability to see has changed from a light-sensitive chemical on a single-celled organism to the extremely complex human eye over three billion years. To get a good idea how many separate steps would be needed (or bases covered), add up the number of colors (seven figures) and multiply each color by every possible intensity. Then, multiply this figure by every possible shape and size, combination, distance, and movement. At least double that figure to coordinate both eyes. And make it happen repeatedly in 200 femtoseconds.

Evolution theory has not identified 99 percent of the intermediate steps between the eyes of an ancient fish and the eyes of a human. It gets even muddier as one goes back to microorganisms. They also cannot explain the very sophisticated eyes of an octopus which descended from a snail-like creature. Or the multifaceted lenses of the dragonfly, the superposition eye of the lobster, or the scanning eye of crabs.

Indeed, there is no proof that most of the required intermediate steps ever existed. Only wishful thinking?

3. OUR PLANET

"The earth from here is a grand oasis
in the big vastness of space."

—ASTRONAUT JIM LOVELL OF **APOLLO 8,**
SPEAKING FROM 250,000 MILES AWAY

As best as astronomers can tell, our planet is one of a kind. There are no other blue marbles with wispy clouds, brown and green continents teeming with life-forms, oceans of water, or radio communications to be found. So far. The universe is a vast place, however, and there may yet be some surprises. If the estimated 14 to 100 million different species living here are truly alone in space, one cannot help wondering if life on Earth is an extraordinary accident, among millions of galaxies, or part of a Plan. Could we merely be varieties of mold, algae, and fungi?

The *anthropic principle* suggests that Earth arrived already set up for life. Whether one believes that or not, there are numerous, incredible coincidences that cannot be easily dismissed. This planet seems to have been placed in the right place, in the right way, at the right time, and carrying all the right ingredients in the right amounts.

Oxygen is a prime example. This is a requirement for life and it has been maintained at a 21 percent plateau for hundreds of millions of years. This precise concentration is critical. If it was nearly absent during the primordial sea days, there are numerous missing links to account for. Where are the intermediate life-forms that needed different and varying amounts of oxygen? Why did oxygen levels plateau at our mandatory level? How did thousands of oxygen-dependent species, without apparent predecessors, explode on the scene 500 to 600 million years ago? These were an odd lot of species, some with five eyes, others with 14 pointed legs, and a few with circular mouths lined by tentacles.

Food or nourishment has also been available from the beginning and we, coincidentally or by Design, have had the right senses to find it, the right anatomy to kill or harvest it, the right gastrointestinal tract to digest it, and the right physiology to benefit. These systems are extremely complex, yet they had to be compatible. Food has been renewable (for example, fruits, roots, and new prey must return every year or so), accessible (not beyond reach), readily identifiable (natural *Open for Business* signs), safe to eat, nutritious, palatable, and potable.

Although it's a simple thought, fruits and vegetables have to ripen first, which is a complex process on its own, and they have a way to make it known when they are ready. When a tomato changes from green to red, a banana changes from hard to soft, or a cantaloupe takes on a sweet scent, they are sending out preprogrammed signals. Imagine how many people would have perished if they had been forced to try out every leaf, flower, bulb, nut, and fruit around, at every stage of development, in hopes that a few would be nutritious. All of life needs to know when their food is ready.

IN THE ZONE

Our home is a planetary safe house. Drs. Gonzalez and Richards, who authored *The Privileged Planet,* call our location in space a narrow habitable zone. Located 150 million kilometers (93 million miles) from the sun, we are far enough away from it to avoid its dangerous emissions, yet close enough to benefit from them. Unlike any other planet, we have the right combination of oxygen and carbon dioxide, the right atmospheric pressures, and water in the right forms in the right places.

The earth's orbit takes us on an unchanging and presumably safe path around the sun. Our lives are protected by complex balances and counterbalances, negative and positive feedback loops, and an inertia. The laws of Nature suit us well, or we suit them well. Minerals are within reach and fire is available to make metals. Shelter can be found or made, and medications might be as close as the mold in your home.

Scientists say the sun is exactly the kind of star that we need. It's very different than the high-mass stars that can be a million times brighter or black holes that would pull us in. Our sun's size, intensity, shape, longevity, orbit, temperature, and position make the Earth very livable. If the sun were barely larger, our planet would be way too hot to support life; a little smaller, way too cold. The sun's rotation within the Milky Way, its control over the other planets, and its safe distance from the closest stars—more than 4.3 light years, or 40 trillion kilometers (25 trillion miles)—keeps our entire solar system stable.

Cosmic Protection

Astronaut Buzz Aldrin, after the *Apollo 11* flight, reported seeing numerous flashes of light inside his eyelids whenever his eyes were closed. These were signs of cosmic rays passing through his brain and hitting retinal cells—a phenomenon called *retinal flashes*. These repeated exposures can destroy a person's brain, and indeed kill. Thus far, they preclude any flight to Mars until a protective technology has been discovered. These same rays would also preclude survival on Earth if we didn't have, as we do, the right atmosphere. Coincidence?

Energy from the sun drives the process of photosynthesis, warms the land and oceans, creates clouds and rain, and emits light waves that allow us to see where we are going and do what we need to do. What would your life be like if our atmosphere were not transparent? The question may sound like a no-brainer, but it is far from it. We do not have echolocation or heat-sensing tongues. Until we invented light, we would have to feel our way to work.

Scientists also say the moon is the right distance away, the right shape, and the right size. It helps keep our 23.5-degree tilt stable, which in turn makes our seasons tolerable, controls our tides, preserves polar ice, and helps prevent drastic temperature changes. The moon gives us light at night. Were it a much darker color, it would absorb, rather than reflect, the light. Were it only found on the sunny side, our nights would be pitch-black.

The earth's size and shape is another good fit. A smaller planet might lose some of our atmosphere or assume a more erratic orbit. A larger planet would, by adding surface area, turn the atmosphere into a gas giant like Jupiter. Our atmosphere has multiple life-sustaining assets. It protects us from the intense cold of space, deadly cosmic rays, and dangerous meteors, yet it allows life-sustaining solar rays to easily pass through. The magnetic field that surrounds the Earth deflects cosmic radiation, solar winds, and the radiation from solar flares. It wraps around us like an invisible blanket.

▦▦ PLANET EARTH ▦▦

Our home in space is safely located in the right planetary order—not too close or too far from the sun, yet far away from any black holes. Most of our planet's surface is water, whose origin cannot be explained by science.

Photo of Earth taken from Apollo 17.[2]

Numerous feedback mechanisms make certain that our planet remains habitable. Every year 20 billion tons of dirty sediment is deposited in the oceans by rivers. Natural systems disperse, distribute, and recycle these particles, keeping our water safe for marine life. A myriad of viruses, bacteria, plant life, mollusks, and scavengers help sanitize the water. If these mechanisms were not in place, we would have had muddy, polluted, and foul-smelling oceans many millennia ago.

Although 450 tons of sodium (salt) are also brought from the mountains to the oceans each year, these bodies of water have maintained the same 3 percent salinity since the beginning. Natural processes link the sodium to other chemicals and then recycle or deposit them elsewhere. All of our fish would die off if the salt concentrations varied year to year or steadily increased.

The atmosphere easily handles an influx of 300 megatons of nitrogen, 100,000 megatons of oxygen, and 140,000 megatons of carbon dioxide per year (megaton = one million tons). Over 1000 megatons of ammonia are produced and neutralized. Millions of tons of methane from the metabolism of microorganisms, industrial pollution, car exhausts, and flatus from both animals and insects are converted into useful chemicals. Carbon dioxide helps create the greenhouse effect, which is not usually a bad thing. Normally, the effect helps keep us warm.

So how are all these balls kept in the air?

THE BIOSPHERES

Life exists in three vastly different biospheres: the hydrosphere or sea, the lithosphere or soil, and the atmosphere or air, which includes all surface beings. Although there is some overlap, the majority of living species spend their entire existence in the same neighborhood. Each locality has its own rules, life-forms, food chains, environment, and ecosystems. All readily suggest ID by their intricate structure, complex physiology, social interactions, constant maintenance, and governing ecology.

Although the three biospheres seem to function separately, each one depends on the success of the other two.

A random thimbleful of sea water has more living organisms than the entire human population, which is presently over six billion. Most species in this thimble are unnamed; indeed, most are still unknown. A cup of soil might have hundreds of miles of fungal threads, millions of bacteria, viruses, insects, crabs, and worms. A cubic mile of air may have as many as 25 million living organisms. Most are molds, bacteria, spores, pollen, and algae catching a ride on the wind to another home, but there can be a number of insects, frogs, fish, and even snakes that have been accidentally blown aloft. History has recorded incidents where towns, much to the residents' dismay, were pelted with fish and frogs. Spiders that normally inhabit lowlands have been found near the top of Mt. Everest. Entomologists assume they were swept up by winds and carried there.

Two miles beneath the Earth's surface there are microorganisms that do not require oxygen, which is a highly unusual paradox. According to scientists they have remained unchanged for three billion years; some say they may even be one of man's first ancestors. How they came about, however, is an enigma—maybe not even from the primordial sea. There are no apparent predecessors, no obvious descendants, and no links.

Self-Regulation

In many ways the planet Earth resembles a living being, and there are a number of contemporary scientists, including James Lovelock and Lynn Margulis, who have written extensively about its impressive, self-regulating physiology. It isn't alive in the usual sense, yet it has been able to actively maintain optimum atmospheric, soil, and oceanic conditions for life as we know it. And it has done so for a very long time.

Fossil records suggest that the Earth's temperatures and climate have remained essentially the same for 3.5 billion years. It cleans, refreshes, protects, defends, regenerates, maintains, and repairs itself.

In a sense, it may breathe, and it definitely has a circulatory system. No one knows how our planet acquired these abilities or remained stable. The only choices appear to be improbable coincidences, Intelligent Design, or incredible luck.

Lovelock calls our planet *Gaia*. The name was taken from the Greek goddess of the Earth, who was nurturing to most people but could also be cruel to those who didn't live in harmony with the planet. This may indeed reflect our distant fate if we continue to pollute the air, damage the coral reefs, mow down the great forests, contaminate our rivers, fight wars with bigger, better weapons, drive plants and animals from their homes and into extinction, treat open lands like garbage dumps, use up natural resources, and intensify the greenhouse effect. Our fertilizers, which have given us more food, and our antibiotics, which have cured many diseases, are also creating hordes of invisible and invincible micromonsters. The sprawling, destructive habits of modern civilization may even be responsible for the increasing severity of hurricanes, tornadoes, forest fires, floods, and global warming. Some think some of these calamities are the Earth trying to correct our errors; others think we're slipping beyond the Earth's ability to clean up our bedrooms.

All is not lost, however. Lovelock points out how durable and stable our planet has been for eons and how carefully it has maintained a very precise concentration of oxygen, carbon dioxide, and nitrogen by balancing the gas exchanges between animals and plants, between the soil and the atmosphere, and between the seas and the atmosphere. It also has backup systems to compensate for any excess or diminished concentrations and it keeps these gases from drifting into outer space. Oxygen and carbon dioxide especially have to be maintained within a narrow range for life to exist. If the oxygen concentration were to drop even a few percentage points, we would all pass out and die; if it were to increase by a mere 4 percent, some experts feel everything that is carbon-based would spontaneously ignite. (FYI—you and I are carbon-based.)

Temperatures at the earth's surface must also be maintained

within a very narrow range for survival. The chill at the North Pole is nothing compared to the freezing temperatures in outer space; a record-setting day in the Sahara Desert cannot come close to temperatures on the sun's surface. Our planet is an odd speck of warmth in a universe that is otherwise incompatible with life. We're like a heat-generating sesame seed in an infinite freezer. The Earth makes use of its ability to retain rather than reflect light; the oceans and carbon dioxide in the atmosphere trap warmth and control the thermostat. When one compares the temperatures at the equator to those at Antarctica, one might think we tolerate a wide range, but this is just a minute variation in the ranges across the universe.

Water Cycles

James Hutton (1726–1797), the father of geology, likened the moving waters on our planet to the circulation of a super organism. Indeed, there are similarities. Water evaporates by the megaton to form massive clouds, which are transported hundreds of miles, where the colder temperatures and higher elevations cause the water to condense and fall back to earth. Water literally flows downhill, gathering in volume and eventually returns to the sea where it will evaporate again. On the way it cleans the air, moderates the climate, weathers the rocks, collects minerals, and fertilizes the valleys.

There are natural mechanisms that constantly cleanse the water. Sunlight and oxygen destroy many of the dangerous microorganisms and toxins. Waves mix up the sediment so decomposition can be hastened. Soil is Nature's filter; it purifies the water as it percolates through the ground. An uncountable number of microorganisms and plants detoxify water by making our poisons their sustenance. Clams and oysters act as siphons or filters at the bottom of the sea. Billions of viruses work as nature's "pool chlorine," killing bacteria in our oceans.

Another set of complex mechanisms maintains a precise salt concentration in our oceans. Our rivers have to be fresh water; our seas salty. Specific mechanisms keep both oxygenated and tightly regulate the concentrations of nutrients, minerals, and gases. These built-in functions adjust life-sustaining processes based on demand, supply, temperatures, depth, and ecology. Without this flexibility our seas would die.

And so would we.

The Earth's surface is 70 percent water. No other planet, that we know of, has anything remotely similar. In addition, scientists do not know where the water came from or why we have such huge oceans. Even the proponents of the Big Bang do not speak of water flying out into space and then recollecting with clumps of dust particles. It had to have come from somewhere. If water is a consequence of millions of years of sunlight decomposing methane, where did all the methane come from? The theory that millions of icy comets struck the earth was tossed out long ago. Comet water has twice as much deuterium as ours.

Water is a perfect fit for life. It's also a huge requirement for all of life and extremely versatile. It comes in three very different forms, liquid, frozen, and vapor, which is unique when compared to other planets. Each natural state has a separate purpose in the scheme of life, and each abides by a different set of chemical and physical laws. According to Michael J. Denton, author of *Nature's Destiny,*

> Without a long chain of vital coincidences in the physical and chemical properties of water, carbon-based life could not exist in any form remotely comparable with that which exists on earth.

The liquid form is the perfect solvent, diluent, and delivery system. Its viscosity helps blood flowing through our arteries and veins. It keeps plant stems turgid and cell walls stiff. It washes our eyes, clears our sinuses, moisturizes our food, makes our skin fresh, keeps mucous membranes from drying up, regulates our internal temperature, and carries away our wastes. It is generally neutral and nontoxic. It's exactly what we (all 14 million species) need for life. Could there have been any intermediate pre-water compounds? If so, no one seems to know what they could have been.

After rain falls at higher elevations, its natural properties of high surface tension and low viscosity (rapid flow) help it remove more than 33 different minerals and carry them to the valleys and seas below. The amount of minerals moved is estimated at 5 billion tons a year. Aquatic life depends on water's constant thermal and chemical controls. They breathe it, swim through it, and see through it. Its high surface tension lends itself to the drawing needs of large plants and trees. Tons of water seem to magically rise through the giant redwoods. Clouds and large bodies of water moderate our weather. It helps make our flowers bloom and our fruits mature.

In its frozen form, water can be stored on mountaintops so that lands below can receive water year-round. In contrast to almost all

---

Who Lit the Match?

According to modern science, somewhere between 10 and 20 billion years ago an atom-sized object with a mass more than a quadrillion times that of our sun suddenly and inexplicably exploded. This event has been called the big bang. Its ejecta have become monstrous fiery balls with temperatures that reach millions of degrees, gargantuan dust clouds, immeasurable amounts of dark matter, and all kinds of planetary debris—including the atoms that make up this very book—all hurtling outward trillions upon trillions of miles at speeds that approached the speed of light. Their movement from the beginning point has been so fast that the actual sound of this explosion has yet to catch up to the fragments. Many of these fragments seem to be racing away from us, which oddly suggests we ought to return to the belief that we are at the center of the universe.

Soon after the big bang, speaking in relative terms, trillions of stars formed galaxies, whose widths span billions upon billions of miles and whose lights continue to shine throughout the cosmos. Interestingly, a few contemporary scientists have constructed descriptions of the first three seconds following the big bang (and, indeed, most of the events of the universe from that moment on). As on the old TV show *Beat the Clock*, that's down from what followed after the first seven minutes, which in turn was an improvement over a description of what happened after the first ten minutes. The chances look very promising that some scientist will soon be able to describe the very first moment and maybe tell us who lit the match. And perhaps even why.

other solids, ice floats. For some odd reason, as temperatures drop, water will contract—and then suddenly around 4° C it will expand before freezing, making it lighter than the liquid form. Just note the ice cubes in your drink, which always come to the top. Other liquids do not convert to a lesser density. This is a life-preserving phenomenon that allows life in lakes and other bodies of water to survive a freezing winter. Imagine how it might be if a lake froze solid from the bottom up. All life therein would perish.

Frank H. Stillinger, an expert on water, is quoted in Michael Denton's book as saying, "It is striking that so many eccentricities should occur together in one substance." John Lewis, a planetary scientist from the University of Arizona, says,

> Despite our best efforts to step aside from terrestrial chauvinism and seek out other solvents and structural chemistries for life, we are forced to conclude that water is the best of all possible solvents and carbon compounds are apparently the best carriers of complex information.

■ ■ ■ ■ ■

How could our planet be so well suited for our needs? Did life self-select and grow into a suit of clothes (an oxygenated and pressurized atmosphere with fresh and salt water), or was this suit of clothes and life designed together?

PART TWO
NATURAL IMPROBABILITIES

Most of us would agree that creatures such as the unicorn and the minotaur are myths. No one has ever proven the existence of a blue-eyed white horse with a single horn or found fossil evidence supporting the existence of an animal whose top half was a bull and bottom half a man (or vice versa). Indeed, we hope to keep it that way.

What if someone were to show that the evolution of the whale, however, was also a myth? Not that whales are fiction, but their life functions are an amazing combination of too many improbable coincidences. This species either skipped over scores of intermediate creatures in its formative stages or added hundreds to thousands of incredibly complex steps simultaneously in one or two generations. To believe they are a product of evolution, we need to be shown remnants of the pre-whales, the pre-pre-whales, and all the other pre-pre's. There are practically none.

The theorists of evolution would like us all to believe that improbable creatures can easily happen, given enough time and enough opportunity. Yet 500 to 600 million years ago, thousands of very weird animals suddenly exploded on the scene. This time period is called the Pre-Cambrian Period, and predecessors to these thousands of animals have rarely, if at all, been found. A couple hundred million years later, extremely huge dinosaurs, monstrous sea creatures, sloths as big as some trees, rhino-types bigger than most trees, eagle-size dragonflies, and giant flying reptiles showed up—again most, if not all, without clear-cut predecessors. Sixty million years later animals with cognitive skills (us?) showed up. To the best of our knowledge, there had not been any cognitive animals beforehand. What a quick improvement, to boot, from thinking whose cave should I pillage today to designing interstellar rockets.

■ ■ ■ ■ ■

Since Darwin's days we have discovered the existence of thousands of new life-forms. Experts say we know of 14 million, but when the seas and microscopic worlds have been finally studied, we could be up to 100 million different species. All of whom should have had several intermediates or predecessors if they were all products of evolution.

Darwin was unaware of microorganisms and, despite the voyage of the *Beagle,* of uncountable numbers of animals found outside of Europe. Darwin had no idea how or why a child looked like his parents or why someone might run a fever when ill. He had never heard of hormones, antibodies, digestive enzymes, neurotransmitters, or insulin. The organisms he knew best were barnacles, earthworms, and local farm animals. The only monkeys he had viewed, according to some historians, were in the zoos, and he only did that twice.

Modern theorists or neo-Darwinists have added numerous single-cell organisms to their evolutionary time line, but the transition stages from no cells to living cells remain unexplained as does the jump to multicellular beings in all biospheres.

4. ON THE LAND

"The love for all living creatures
is the most noble attribute of man."

—CHARLES DARWIN

The mere act of walking, crawling, galloping, hopping, slithering or, indeed, any form of locomotion could not have come about after a few accidental, sequential steps (links). Having one leg when two are needed is useless (or three versus four). Having a hand without a blood supply would be a hindrance. Although a rare type of fin can be found on a few fish that can "walk" along the sea bottom, these appendages are anatomically very different than legs. Darwin's theories make the changes look easy, but the truth is, the transition from swimmer to walker requires millions of steps and impossible coincidences. Below are just a few standout examples.

THE PLATYPUS

This incredible web-footed mammal from Australia and Tasmania is one of only two mammals that lay eggs. It also lacks teeth. Platypuses are often called duckbills because of a hairless snout that has a remarkable resemblance to a duck's bill, not a mammal's snout. In fact, when Europeans first viewed this animal's carcass, they insisted it was a fake, that someone had sewn the bill of a duck to a large mole. This bill, however, is unmatched in biology. After closing its eyes and ears, the platypus uses this bill to create an electrical field to find shrimp, worms, and other bottom life. No billed animal is known to create an electrical field. The only other mammal that lays eggs is the echidna.

■■ PLATYPUS ■■

The platypus is a *mosaic* animal that, according to current scientific reckoning, dates back millions of years. It lacks any clear-cut ancestors. Since it is an egg-laying mammal with milk glands and a leathery duckbill, present evolutionary reasoning might say it is evolving into a duck.

© *Tom McHugh / Photo Researchers, Inc.*[3]

Other unparalleled characteristics include a hollow spur behind each ankle in the males. They look like fangs and are connected to poison glands that can seriously injure anyone who handles the animal. Because these spurs enlarge during mating, some biologists think they are part of the fight for a lady companion. Another unprecedented characteristic is how the babies get their milk. It is secreted like sweat by numerous glands on the mother's abdomen, where the newborns lap it up.

Laying eggs is reptilian; being warm-blooded and nursing is mammalian. Where are the cold-blooded predecessors with or without electrical snouts or poisonous spurs?

THE CORPSE FLOWER

This unique plant from Sumatra grows to a height of nine feet and a width of four feet. It produces a huge, foul-smelling "flower" that shoots up from its center. The fragrance is barely tolerable to humans, resembling something between rotting eggs and the remains of a dying animal. This scent, however, is highly attractive to carrion beetles, dung beetles, flies, and wasps who pollinate it. Although every corpse flower has male and female flowers at the base of the spath (the "flower"), they mature at different rates and cannot self-pollinate.

The stench disappears rather quickly, and the spath collapses exposing the seeds. The plant's flesh becomes attractive to birds, who will carry and deposit the seeds elsewhere in a pile of droppings.

THE COCKROACH

Nearly everything about the cockroach defies the theory of evolution. Relatively speaking, this insect may be the toughest species around. It certainly is the most enduring, having been on Earth, essentially unchanged, for about 350 million years. One would think it had plenty of time to evolve way beyond us, perhaps be flying spaceships to distant galaxies by now. Nonetheless, cockroaches may also be among the smartest nonhumans around. Researchers who challenge animals to solve mazes say that a cockroach is nearly as smart as an octopus, which ranks right below dolphins and chimps.

Cockroaches eat almost anything, live just about anywhere, and survive nearly everything that man and Nature can throw at them. They may even become the last survivors of this planet. Some experts think they could survive a nuclear blast. Perhaps not precisely at ground zero, where even dirt dies, but they may well be the first and closest living beings to return. The lethal dose of radiation for a human is less than 1000 rads over a few weeks, whereas a laboratory cockroach can survive 9600 rads over five weeks.

Despite our universal aversion to these creatures, the feelings are not mutual. Cockroaches like what we eat, especially the items we discard; they like what we read (to eat, not peruse); they love the treats we leave out in fruit bowls, candy dishes, and pet dishes; they enjoy traveling wherever we go—nothing better than the crevice inside a suitcase to Bimini; and they love our homes, hotels, businesses, and restaurants. Despite all their affection for us, they have never made good pets.

There are over 3500 identified species of cockroaches, but that number will likely top 5000, since new varieties are found every year. They range in size from one-tenth of an inch to nearly four inches. Some are small enough to hitch a ride on the backs of leafcutter ants. Florida holds the gold medal for the most species, while Texas owns silver. They are related to mantids and grasshoppers and can be identified by leathery forewings, an egg purse, and certain mouth parts.

Their anatomy is amazingly complex. Their exterior is covered with a very durable—yet multijointed and very flexible—suit of armor that is no thicker than a hair's width. It hardens within hours of their birth. Later, when they outgrow it, they will suck in enough air to break the seams, eat the busted pieces (remember, they eat nearly everything), suck in air again to maximize their size, and then secrete a new coating that quickly hardens and tans. The process is called molting, and it happens about five to seven times over their life span. It keeps moisture in and bacteria out and it is manipulated by more muscles than we have. This is an all-or-none phenomenon, as a half a coat is half too short. A delay in the hardening process can make them very vulnerable (and more ugly).

They run on three legs alternating the front and back leg on one side paired with the middle leg on the other side. If one compares distance covered compared to body length, relatively speaking, they are three times faster than a cheetah. One species has a special tongue to absorb water vapor from the air. Although they eat decaying wood, none of them can actually digest wood without special protozoa in their gut (similar to termites). These symbiotic microorganisms are passed from parents to offspring.

Their antennae have 130 segments; they have bristles for grooming, and they can easily sense temperature, motion, and anything edible. They have special mouthparts similar to crab claws, which check out the food before they bite into it. They also have a second set of teeth in their stomachs to finish the job. Their legs have a ball and socket joint similar to a human hip and a hinge joint like our knees. They have two brains, one in the head and one near their behind. This may be why they can live for weeks if their head is cut off.

Hissing cockroaches from Madagascar actually do hiss like cats do, to deter predators. They are able to reach 70 decibels, louder than casual conversation, and they can be heard at 12 feet. It seems that hissing could not have come about in intermediate steps (links). Imagine a prehistoric cockroach trying a low-decibel grunt or hiss in the face of a dangerous predator. Hissing under one's breath, one would guess, was less than useful. To be effective, it had to have been done in the right way, the first time, accompanied by the right body language.

Despite being avid groomers, cockroaches are attracted to garbage and excrement. They live among trash and excrement, and they enjoy eating all types of human and animal waste. Sewers are one of their favorite hangouts, and cleaning up the planet is truly their job. The downside is the obvious—they pick up and carry nearly every disease found in sewers. This, of course, explains most of our aversions. Their gifts that keep on giving include hepatitis, dysentery, and polio. The polio epidemic in the 1950s may well have been spread more by cockroaches than people.

Cockroaches do not get ill from these pathogens. Like one of us carrying dog hair or cat dander on our clothes, they inadvertently transport these infectious agents on their legs and external casing to your food, kitchen countertops, children's toys, bedding, toothbrushes, and restaurants. Viruses, bacteria, fungi, spores, and specks of urine and feces literally fall off or rub off wherever they go. Cockroaches may be good for recycling waste, but due to their massive numbers and frequent need to expel gas, they are also a major contributor to methane levels and the greenhouse effect.

Contrary to evolutionary thought about survival of the fittest, certain male cockroaches, like the Tanzanian species, select partners with the lowest social rank and produce the lowest possible number of offspring. The more inferior, the more appealing. Why?

Many other questions arise. Where is the precedent for a second brain or the second set of teeth in the stomach? How did 130 segments in the antennae evolve—one at a time or all at once? How could the whole mechanism of molting the old coat and secreting the new coat come about in intermediate steps? It's sort of like ripping your clothes off during a teenage growing spurt and then running around in your birthday suit for a few hours while someone makes you new clothes.

THE ELEPHANT

This five-ton animal is another improbable creature. Their trunks ("noses") can be 10 t0 13 feet long, and there are no predecessors with "prototrunks." Approximately 60,000 muscles coordinate such diverse activities as lifting a few strands of hay, pulling down trees, snorkeling when swimming, spraying their bodies with dirt or water, checking a female's urine for estrus, scribbling with a pencil, and trumpeting information. They can also send subsonic communications hundreds of miles and seem to recognize themselves in a mirror.

Considerable design has gone into this animal. A deer this size would collapse. If its head were any larger, it could not be held up. Everything about its bony structure is appropriate for its massive size—lighter bones on top, heavier below. If its head, already close to a ton, were any larger or its neck longer, it would topple forward. It has cushions beneath its feet to help support its weight. Its teeth are huge, able to chew acacia branches four inches in diameter, thorns and all. The incisors become tusks, another unusual phenomenon; each may weigh hundreds of pounds and reach ten feet. Tusks help collect food, threaten predators or rivals, and show sexual prowess. And contrary to nearly all other mammals, elephants are bald.

THE EMPEROR PENGUIN

This very unusual bird has survived an incredibly harsh life for thousands of years. Fossils indicate it once stood eight feet tall, and some scientists think it evolved from the albatross. If so, one must look closely at what had to have simultaneously changed in a bird that can fly for days over vast expanses of water, even around the world, to a flightless bird that can hold its breath 15 minutes and dive 1500 meters (a third of a mile) deep in frigid water. One would have to speculate the improbable: that successive generations slowly lost their wings, gained knowledge of the cold sea, learned how to track food underwater, shifted their physiology to maximize oxygen usage, adjusted to the pressures of deep water, avoided the bends, and learned how to breed during the Antarctic winter.

The emperor penguin now stands closer to four feet. Every year some groups march (walk and slide in unison) 70 miles to their birthplace to reproduce. No one knows how they find the exact spot among endless, changing, white icy shelves or how the chosen ones are chosen. This is a very particular spot that is close to the water's shore during the warmer months but far enough away during the coldest (breeding) weather. They are monogamous and very caring. The male will hold an egg in his pouch for two-and-a-half months during periods where temperatures drop to 100 degrees below zero with 100-mph winds; males rotate their positions among the inner and outer circles to keep warm.

The female leaves after laying the egg and transferring it to a pouch above the father's feet—which in itself is an incredible accomplishment that is fraught with danger to the embryo. During the next 125 days of incubation, the father goes without eating and loses half his weight. Somehow the returning mother is able to find the right father and egg among hundreds; she always arrives within a few days of its hatching. Nonetheless, the father keeps a snack for the hatchling in its gullet to tide the newborn over just in case the mother can't make it back quite on time. (How would that happen with evolution?)

The mother brings partially digested fish in a stomach pouch for the youngster; nobody knows how she keeps it from spoiling. Meanwhile, the father leaves to feed himself. Before departing he seems to give his youngster some unique signal so they can find each other. Later on, the offspring also leave the birthing area as a group, without any of the adults, and go to sea for four to five years. Nobody knows how they know where to go or when to return.

Why would any animal, intent on surviving, have their young at the most hazardous time of the year in the Antarctic? How do they find the right place every time? And how did they come so well equipped for this environment?

All improbable coincidences that lack precedents.

THE FLEA

The flea can jump into the air faster than the human eye can see. In fact, it can jump for three days at hundreds of times an hour with accelerations of 100G, presumably thinking it will land on something or someone worthwhile. Their bite will inject saliva, which contains a blood thinner (anticoagulant) and a blood-vessel dilator (vasodilator), opening up the blood vessels and keeping them from clotting so that they can freely suck up the blood. Without this combination, their meal would be sparse.

THE BEAVER

Beavers are fascinating engineers without rival or predecessor. Somehow, a beaver couple will know how to dam up a stream to make a home in the middle of a body of water to protect themselves from bears and lynx. This lodge can be as large as 100 feet long and 10 feet tall. Their incredibly strong incisors can gnaw through trees as thick as 20 inches, and then, using a powerful paddlelike tail, the beavers drag the limbs up- or downstream. Gaps in their home are filled in with mud, reeds, stones, and twigs. They sleep on a ledge above water and use an underwater entrance. This home even has vents for gases to escape. If the water level behind the dam gets too high (potentially flooding their home) or too low (allowing predators a muddy access route), they will make adjustments in their dam to keep the water level exactly where they want it to be.

Where are the intermediate home-builders?

This animal has transparent eyelids or goggles, flaps to protect its ears from freezing water, and a flap in the throat to protect back teeth. When their front teeth grind down, they regrow. And they have a unique lubrication on their fur to keep them warm and dry.

To survive as land-dwelling creatures, every animal species, from the tiniest soil microbes to the giant mammoth, would have had to have passed through millions of intermediary steps (links)…which are thus far unaccounted for in the scientific documents.

5. IN THE SEA

"Collectively, the oceans form a reservoir of
dissolved gases which help regulate the
composition of the air we breathe and to
provide a stable environment for marine
life—about half of all living matter."

— J.E. LOVELOCK, PHD
AUTHOR OF GAIA: A NEW LOOK AT LIFE ON EARTH

Maintaining normal bodily functions despite enormous external pressures, regulating buoyancy, extracting oxygen from seawater, safely reproducing, and skillfully swimming are not abilities that sea animals could have acquired after a few accidental changes over the millennia. Examples that require millions, maybe billions, of well-coordinated genetic interactions can be found everywhere. A few of these impossible coincidences are described below.

NUDIBRANCHS

Nudibranchs (meaning "naked gills"), or sea slugs, are beautiful creatures that are essentially underwater snails without shells. They have the incredible ability to safely swallow *nematocysts* (packets of nerve toxins) as they feed on sea anemones, coral, and jellyfish, and then move them through their body to their outer tips *(cerata)* to be used as defense mechanisms. This would be like a person swallowing several small pistols and then having them pop out in their hands, loaded and ready to fire. Some are even strongly scented or brightly colored to warn predators of their toxicity. Also, their gills have an added flap to protect them when they are buried in sand.

Certain tropical nudibranchs can store algae in their cerata so that they have a continuous supply of manufactured sugars. Others selectively ingest pigments from algae and sponges, and move them to their surface to camouflage themselves. Each nudibranch is a hermaphrodite, and when they mate, each passes a sperm sac to the other. Self-fertilization is rare, but appears to be in place for backup.

THE OCTOPUS

Not only is the octopus unique, but it is one of the more interesting species in the sea; it certainly is one of the smartest. It functions with "distributed intelligence," meaning that its thinking occurs both in the brain as well as in billions of neurons distributed along its tentacles. This design works very well for such needs as reaching into darkened crevices and tearing open clam shells. Imagine the benefit if we could do the same. A student could do homework with one hand and play video games with the other. No one knows how this distributed thinking skill came about.

The suckers work together or alone; the pull can vary from incredibly gentle to strong enough to hoist the animal out of an aquarium. Night watchmen have reported seeing octopi sneak out of their quarters, slip into other aquariums, make a feast of the occupants (usually crabs), and scamper back home before the daytime employees arrive.

They are one of very few animals that have observational intelligence. One classic experiment had a group of octopi watching (from their separate aquariums) while another octopus would receive food whenever it played with a red ball, not a yellow ball. Overwhelmingly, the octopi observers selected the red ball when they were given their turn.

Octopi are also very versatile. They can change color to fit their environment, change color to reflect their emotions (red for anger and white for fear), and change shapes for offense or defense. They can mimic a flounder, a coconut, or a snake. Some octopi as large as ten feet across can slip through a one-and-a-half-inch pipe.

One aspect that particularly defies evolution theory is the fact that every mother octopus dies very soon after her babies are born. The hatchlings are literally on their own. Except for moments during pro-creation, they live a solo life, yet they somehow know from the very start how to carry out their lives. This is an all-or-none phenomenon.

Most of the intermediate links to the octopus appear to be missing.

THE DOLPHIN

The dolphin is another very curious and likable species. Despite living in the seas and having some features that resemble fish, they are not fish. Not even close. They are warm-blooded mammals who bear their young alive and nurse their offspring. There are no gills, scales, eggs, or swim bladders. Their tails move up and down rather than sideways; they have complex communication systems; they breathe air just as we do; and their brains are much larger than any fish the same size.

These animals are highly streamlined, sometimes called living torpedoes, and perfectly shaped to maximize their speed—like a racing car or jet fighter. Their smooth exterior design is so well honed to lessen drag that even their nipples and genitals are tucked away. Dolphins can reach speeds of 25 mph and easily dive to 300 meters for 20 minutes. Some have been seen as deep as 1500 feet.

Dolphins live within a sleek, lubricated wet suit that is insulated with thick, flexible blubber that may also give their tail muscles an extra counterbounce. Oddly, they shed their skin every two hours. Like humans, they maintain an internal temperature of 37° C (98.6° F), but whenever diving, their physiology automatically accommo-dates the increasing pressure and dropping external temperatures by altering bloodflow to less vital areas. They do not suffer from the bends.

Each eye has nearly 180-degree vision, able to see food or predators above, below, or virtually anywhere in their vicinity, both in and out of water. At times, they view others with one eye. The nearly extinct and virtually blind river dolphin that is found (and threatened) in a small, polluted stretch of the Yangtze River is born with both eyes in the right location. They soon migrate upward, however, which according to evolution theory, is to gather more light. Moving an eyeball would be similar to moving a lung. It's not a simple process. Why not be born with the eyes on top of the head?

A dolphin's back and fluke tail are very flexible and powerful. This gives them a distinct advantage when hunting for food. They dive faster than most fish and can attack prey from any position. Their nostril or blowhole is precisely placed on the top of their head to surface-breathe. Had it ever been under the chin or beside the head, best guess is that the lineage would never have lasted.

They start the process of exhalation an instant before they surface by opening a tightly plugged nostril. They expel an explosive jet stream of droplets and air, and once safely above the waterline, rapidly suck in enough air. The latter is accomplished in less than a second.

Dolphin babies are born after 14 months of gestation. When they arrive they must be ready to swim, surface for breathing, and follow their mother. They are among the largest babies compared to the mother's size. Dolphins nurse with a frilled tongue that forms a seal. Milk, which is richer than human milk, is squirted into their mouths.

Dolphins are very social animals. They travel in groups, fight in groups, hunt in groups, pair up to steal females, and commit suicide by beaching in groups. They seem to know consequences of their behaviors. For example, mothers will form small groups that allow one mother to seek food while the other protect the offspring. They have many ways to communicate, including clicks, whistles, pops, and certain sounds we can't hear. All convey specific information. Sometimes they seem to stay in touch just to be sure they are all still close by to each other.

Dolphins have incredible abilities to regenerate parts of their body. They endure numerous bites, lacerations, and tears—wounds humans might not survive without a very quick trip to the emergency room. Instead of a clot they form an impenetrable shield and then a scar beneath.

According to the theory of evolution, dolphins are not direct descendants of fish. Instead, they began as warm-blooded land animals that returned to the sea many millions of years ago and have not changed one iota in five million years. No one knows how a transition to deep diving, sleek exteriors, temperature maintenance, pressurization, midline blowholes, different food, different predators, plus having offspring who immediately know how to breathe at the surface, could have ever come about.

PFIESTERIA

This one-celled marine organism is sometimes called the "cell from hell." It is a weird species of the algae family that is called dinoflagellates because of two whiplike tails or flagella. Pfiesteria (Fist-TEAR-e-ah) act like an animal sometimes and a plant at other times; it is responsible for the Eastern Seaboard's algae blooms that kill millions of fish and other sea life every year. They can also be caustic and sometimes fatal to a person who swims in, drinks, touches, or even breathes near the contaminated water.

Pfiesteria are different than the usual algae blooms that cause brown and red tides elsewhere. These organisms are colorless, unpredictable, and extremely aggressive. Something about the scent of a passing school of fish, perhaps their oily skin or excrement, will set these dinoflagellates off by the billions. They immediately release volumes of two toxins. The first one is a nerve toxin; it stuns the passing fish. The second

The Starry Batfish

This is a rather newly discovered species found at a depth of 1200 feet near the Hawaiian Islands. It looks like an orange disc slightly bigger than a Frisbee, with two eyes up front, a long tail, and thorny exterior made of interlocking bony plates. It walks on four fins that resemble legs, or swims—and it can propel itself with jet squirts from gill slits on both sides. No one knows how this one came about.

weakens their immunity and produces deep sores. The dying tissues and blood become a feast.

What's least explainable by the theory of evolution is their ability to change shapes. They can change from a semidormant cyst in the seabed sediment to a mobile fish killer within hours. These cysts are nearly indestructible—for example, they can withstand full-strength hydrochloric acid for 30 minutes. Twenty different forms are known, including the cyst, an amoeba shape, a star shape, and a torpedo type with two whiplike tails. No one knows how they do it, where they came from, and what to do about them. There are algae and non-algae predecessors, but nobody knows how they got together to pull off this number.

CICHLIDS

The cichlids are a group of fish found in certain African lakes. Darwinists call them the darlings of evolution. It's their rapid rate of speciation (ability to evolve) that is cited as comparable to Darwin's famous finches on the Galápagos Islands. These fish have variable mating and parenting systems that depend, in part, on their environment. They are universally monogamous, which is highly unusual for fish, and they have adaptable parenting skills, which include carrying the eggs around in their mouth. Females can change their sex whenever there's a shortage of males. The adults will even allow the offspring to feed off their flesh if food is in short supply.

Numerous items are daunting for Darwinists despite labeling this species a great example of evolution. Perhaps that flexibility is already built in. For example, cars retain the ability to go in reverse should the need arise. The idea that any animal can change its sex must have required uncountable evolutionary steps (links) that have yet to be discovered. This is much more than the changing of one's jacket or cologne; it's a retrofit or activation of the male organs and a deactivation of anything female.

Another vexing characteristic is the cichlid's caring for other species' fry (babies). According to Darwin himself, anything that indicates one species will help another, other than the use of domesticated animals, contradicts survival of the fittest. Cichlids will round up, care for, and raise fry as their own from entirely different fish species. Often this is a consequence of a territorial fight.

■ ■ ■ ■ ■

None of these examples could have evolved by partial measures. Partial fins or incomplete gills would never have been compatible with survival underwater. If water species came about through ways suggested by the theory of evolution, the changes would have required millions, at a minimum, of intracellular changes en route.

Where are they? The answer is, they don't exist and will never be found.

6. IN THE AIR

> "Although the feather is a symbol of lightness, feathers still account for between 15 and 20 percent of a bird's total weight. A bird's skeleton, by contrast, is often less than half of the weight of the feathers."
>
> —THE SIBLEY GUIDE, NATIONAL AUDUBON SOCIETY

A life that includes flying needs to have arrived in a single package, not via sequential steps, such as jumping or controlled falling out of trees. If a species doesn't have all the complexities needed to take off into the air, stay aloft, and safely land, it will never survive…just as eggs without a very sophisticated internal timing mechanism would never hatch. The acquisition and retention of these abilities defy the simple, untested answers offered by theorists of evolution. Below are just a few of the many impressive examples.

THE BAT

Bat fossils that remarkably resemble modern bats are dated back to 50 million years ago, but no apparent predecessor species has been found. Biologists speculate that the bat's ancestors might have been tree-dwelling shrews or moles who had some capability to glide, but that's mere conjecture. It doesn't explain echolocation, which is their sonar ability to find food on the wing at night, or how they can purposefully drop their body temperatures at night to save energy. Most mammals constantly burn energy to maintain a specific temperature 24/7.

According to Charles Kingsley Levy, from the moment a bat's

echolocation picks up an insect to the time of kill is less than 4 seconds. If compared, by size, to our sonar detectors, theirs is one trillion times more efficient. Bats can fly at speeds up to 60 mph and at heights of 10,000 feet. Often they live in caves by the millions. Nurseries may have as many as 2000 pups per square meter, yet mom always seems to know her offspring. Their young nurse on breasts much like all mammals.

One interesting capability that breaks the rules of the theory of evolution is their ability to lock onto a rock and hang upside down without falling. This is made possible by an automatic locking mechanism in their feet. A tendon closes the toes against the rock, and then the bat's weight creates the proper tension downward to keep it locked. The moment the bat grabs the rock the clamping mechanism snaps in place. The unprecedented backward-facing knees with forward-facing feet aid the process.

Bats will sleep and carry on most of their necessary activities in a hanging position for hours, only flipping 180 degrees whenever there's a need to evacuate their bladder or defecate. One might feel sorry for the predecessors who had not yet learned to flip over.

When it's time to hunt for food, they just release, drop, and take off. Partially-hanging, sometimes-falling intermediates did not exist.

THE WOODPECKER

The common woodpecker, one would think, could not be an impossible consequence of evolution, yet there are many improbable coincidences that presently lack good explanations.

First, their beak was designed to break through hard wood. Would a softer beak in ancient time been effective? Or a downward curved one? According to Dr. Jobe Martin, that beak is industrial-strength, supported by the thickest skull bones around. The beak also has a cartilaginous cushion at its base, protecting the head from the trauma (like foam-rubber gloves to handle a jackhammer). Two front toes and two in back, different than other birds, plus elastic tail feathers, form a tripod to help secure the bird to a spot on the tree. It remains in absolute perfect position to do what it must do. They close their eyes with each peck, presumably to prevent wood chips from causing damage, or to keep their eyes from popping out, or both.

Once the hole is made or widened, a unique tongue, which is longer than its beak, penetrates tiny holes in search of insects. This tongue has rear-facing barbs and a sticky glue that, for reasons related to Design, does not stick to the inside of the bird's beak. A solvent inside the bird quickly frees the attached victim, the insect is swallowed whole, and the tongue goes back to work. In some species the tongue comes out between the eyes. The European green woodpecker takes it a step further. It has a tongue that goes around inside its head and out between its eyes.

The theory of evolution cannot explain any of this.

OTHER INEXPLICABLE EXAMPLES

The pelican's nostril has a flap that closes when it dives. Kiwi birds sniff along the ground like a dog, and they are the only bird with nostrils at the tip of their beak. There are studies that suggest these birds essentially *inhale* a map, just as we would visually memorize a route home. Some seabirds, like the petrels and prions, can smell DMS (dimethyl sulfide) in the seas. This is where they will find a meal of krill who are feasting on zooplankton and phytoplankton. Pigeons must also use smell; with their nasal passages blocked, they cannot find their way home as easily as those whose nostrils are not blocked.

The red knot bird flies nearly 9000 miles each year to feast on millions of horseshoe crab eggs laid along Delaware's coast. Within ten days, the female lays four large eggs. All this is described by ornithologist Brian Harrington: "It is no exaggeration to liken her accomplishment to a woman giving birth to a sixty-pound baby within ten days of completing a six-thousand mile hike at altitudes higher than the Himalayas!"

■■■■■

Just as we cannot fly from Los Angeles to Tokyo in a jet with a single left wing, a half-empty fuel tank, improper pressurization, or a faulty guidance system, a species that makes use of flight must also have flight-ready anatomy, physiology, and instincts from its beginnings. None of these are simple steps; none could have merely come about by gradual transition. Imagine a jet with a normal left wing and a tiny right wing—and then the next generation, assuming it survived, having half a normal right wing. The number of missing links in this area of study is huge.

7. SUBTERRANEAN LIFE

"The thousands of species of bacteria found in the top two soil horizons play a vital role in the biogeochemical cycling of elements that is important to the sustainability of all life on the planet."

—DAVID W. WOLFE, PhD,
AUTHOR OF **TALES FROM THE UNDERGROUND**

Five hundred years ago Leonardo da Vinci said, "We know more about the movement of celestial bodies than the soil underfoot." His statement still rings true today. Despite its obvious proximity we know very little about life beneath us. Yet this dark, seemingly silent world is crisscrossed by trillions of miles of fungal threads, penetrated by quintillions of root hairs, and inhabited by a near-infinite number of viruses, bacteria, molds, fungi, protozoa, insects, crabs, worms, reptiles, and mammals. A pinch of soil can have a billion or more lives, each of them incredibly complex on their own, every system governed by unique rules. Their survival may or may not be dependent on us, but ours is clearly locked into their well-being.

The legume family, which includes peas, beans, peanuts, alfalfa, many foraging plants, and thousands of flowering species, is a good example of complex underground life systems. Every plant requires the presence of specific soil bacteria to extract and fix (meaning change, not repair) forms of nitrogen from dead organic matter and animal wastes. They cannot make any of their life-sustaining proteins without fixed nitrogen. We cannot live without their proteins. Meanwhile, the bacteria benefit also from nutrients taken away from the plant's root system.

Author David Wolfe writes the following in *Tales from the Under-ground:*

> We and all other life forms on the planet, including most microbes, depend on a special group of prokaryote (bacteria and archaea) species called "nitrogen fixers" to convert N_2 gas into something the rest of us can use. The evolutionary "invention" of nitrogen fixation ranks with photosynthesis (carbon fixation) as one of the cornerstone events in the history of life on Earth.

One might ask how plants could have "evolved" without the ability to recover nitrogen. Surely, survival of the fittest should have brought out more autonomous groups. For some reason it didn't, and interestingly, it can't be just any plant using any nitrogen-fixing bacteria. There are very particular compatibility issues. Somehow, the right bacteria is capable of finding the right root, and both it and the root know how to set up a mutually beneficial shop without ever having seen each other before. To date, scientists have found over 20 genes that aid in this process.

THE EARTHWORM

In *The Earth Moved,* Amy Stewart wrote that earthworms are the custodians of the planet, meaning they take care of the soil for all living beings. Hundreds to thousands of worms can sometimes be found in a handful of soil, and they live virtually everywhere. Anything dead already has or certainly will have worms in it soon. If you look at any vegetable or fruit close enough, you will probably find a worm or two. If, for some odd reason, the dirt of the earth were washed away, according to Nathan Cobb, who is a pioneer in the science of nematodes, every continent would be covered with a thick film of wriggling worms.

Some of Darwin's best work may have been done with earthworms. He once wrote, "The plough is one of the most ancient and most valuable of man's inventions, but long before he existed, the land was, in fact, regularly ploughed, and still continues to be thus ploughed by earth-worms." Darwin spent hours observing them and recorded how they could draw certain pine needles into their holes. He tried to prove they could hear and see, and he wrote about them extensively in *The Formation of Vegetable Mould, Through the Action of Worms, With Observations on Their Habits* (1881).

Although many of Darwin's research techniques are now known to be flawed, he was correct in many ways about the importance of earthworms. They are constantly preparing the soil for farming. They consume about a third of their body weight daily, loosening up the soil so roots can go deeper, and altering its capacity to hold water. They add nutrients by way of their enriched castings and participate in the recycling process by chewing up much of the downed vegetation. Although the volume of an individual cast may fill a tablespoon, worms may produce 20 to 30 tons of castings per acre.

One can take a seat in the forest and literally watch leaves being pulled into holes. Chemically damaged forests—meaning chemically damaged worms too—will steadily collect leaves, pile up debris, and slowly die. In a terrarium, one can see worms shred vegetable debris and expel them as biologically active castings. The incredible fertility of the Nile Valley is attributed to thousands of tons of castings over thousands of years.

According to fossil studies, worms have been here for nearly half a billion years. Like fish who are designed to swim through the ocean and birds to fly in the sky, they are designed to wriggle (swim?) through the soil. A pointed head penetrates crevices moistened by its own spit while circular muscles squeeze the organism smaller and longitudinal muscles flex and extend. They can easily go forward and backward, hibernate for years several feet under the ground, and have enormous capabilities to regenerate lost parts.

If an earthworm has the misfortune of running into a predator that bites off its head, it instinctively writhes backward, hurries off, and soon grows another head or any other injured part. Worms can be cut into pieces and every segment will grow another worm. Cut the worm at segment 18 and it will grow exactly 18 segments back and add the appropriate head or tail. One can suture the tail from one worm with the middle section from another and a head from a third, and they will soon function as a new worm. Try connecting the dots on this evolutionary game. Impossible?

Although they lack lungs or gills, worms can breathe through their skin. Their blood contains hemoglobin which is similar to the oxygen-carrying protein moiety in humans, but it can carry more oxygen more easily. They have one to five hearts in a row and a primitive brain. They can sense the moisture in soil and adjust their depth. They can also sense light except when busy copulating.

Highly varied and skilled subterranean organisms undo the dead and restart the living. Earthworms might be considered the bulldozers in recycling organic matter, but they are preceded by or accompanied by battalions of pulverizing arthropods (insects like mites, beetles, and springtails) who are preceded by or accompanied by armies of bacteria, fungi, and protozoa that cause decay. It is almost like putting your garbage can out in front of your house, any time, any day, and having the disposal company show up immediately, acting as if it were a 9-1-1 call.

Most earthworms depend on microorganisms, some external to the deceased, to start the decomposition process, and others inside their digestive tracts to aid the process. There are some instances where the earthworms have carried disease-causing bacteria to different fields. Some earthworms, like the *Eisenia fetida,* cannot reproduce without a specific protozoan in their gut.

Many worms are hermaphrodites, meaning every worm contains both sex organs, which are actually sexual pores. They reproduce by lining up along-side one another, head to tail, and anchoring themselves with tiny bristles and a sticky body fluid. Seminal fluid leaves the male pores and is moved along a longitudinal groove by muscular contractions to the opposing female pores, one pore at a time. The eggs are not fertilized immediately, however. Sperm and eggs are placed in a mucus shell that hardens into a cocoon about the size of a very small, lemon-shaped marble. Then the end seals off as the parent pulls away. This cocoon will automatically postpone the fertilization process if conditions outside, like hot or dry weather, are not acceptable. The giant Australian worm leaves a cocoon the size and shape of a lemon that may not allow fertilization for a year. These are very complex steps for a seemingly simple species to follow.

Another very significant worldwide underground symbiotic system belongs to the huge family of mycorrhizal fungi. They may be the oldest living species on earth and one of the most extensive. A wood-digesting fungus, *Armillaria bulbosa,* which can be found in a Michigan forest, is estimated to be the size of several football fields and weigh more than 100 tons. Fortunately, it's underground and not walking around. No one truly knows how old it is, but educated guesses make it to be many thousands of years old.

Mycorrhizal networks are responsible, in large part, for the health of 90 percent of crop plants, fruit trees, forests, and wildflowers. In exchange for the nutrients they recover from sap, which is mostly products of photosynthesis, they decompose local organic materials and convey those breakdown products along with water through highly complex pipelines to plants. Although there may be an occasional compatibility issue, these organisms are not nearly as selective as the nitrogen-fixing bacteria. They may even connect to several different varieties of plants at the same time.

Life in the Depths

The underground ecosystems are not like the vertical food chains found on the surface. Most of subterranean life occurs in the litter layer or topsoil—in contrast to clay/part humus below sixteen inches and clay/rock below three feet—but specialized sterile drilling techniques have found unique microorganisms at much deeper levels that do not depend on the usual requirements of sunlight and oxygen. In fact, very different microbes have been found at a depth of two miles in the gold mines of South Africa. A restudied group of microorganisms called *methanogens* may be responsible for most, if not all, of the methane or natural gas that is found within the depths of our earth. It appears to be a byproduct of bacterial metabolism over the eons. A convenient Design? There are no apparent predecessors.

■ ■ ■ ■ ■

The complexities of underground life and the countless number of unidentified, interacting species defy the sequential or accidental changes proposed by evolution. Every modern study indicates that the more science learns about the subterranean world, the more Darwin's explanations become untenable.

8. THE MICROBIAL AND SUBMICROBIAL WORLD

"The greatest of all accomplishments of twentieth-century science has been the discovery of human ignorance."

—LEWIS THOMAS, PHYSICIAN,
AUTHOR OF **THE LIVES OF A CELL**

Microorganisms are critical to all aspects of life on our planet. They are largely responsible for the presence, maintenance, and recycling of oxygen, nitrogen, phosphorus, and carbon. They destroy toxins and convert waste products into crucial nutrients, and they recycle the remains of dead animals and plants. Imagine how our world might look without the mechanisms of decay. Also, if it were not for microorganisms converting unusable nitrogen compounds in the soil into an essential chemical nutrient for plant growth, we would not have food on our tables. There would not be forests if it weren't for the nearly infinite underground networks of fungi that provide nutrients to tree roots.

One-celled organisms are considered by evolutionists to be among the oldest living entities on our planet; they may easily be the dominant living force. Their numbers alone are staggering, far beyond quintillions; there may be hundreds of thousands of species, most of which are not yet catalogued. Some scientists estimate there are ten million species on earth and the vast majority are virtually invisible.

The second smallest living group is the mycoplasm that weighs in at 0.0000000000001 grams. Add a few more zeros after the decimal for the size of a virus. It would take 300 average-sized bacteria, laid out side by side, to achieve the width of the period at the end of this sentence. Despite a single organism's minuscule weight, if all microorganisms were weighed together they would outweigh all other living beings combined. Billions can be found in a handful of soil; nearly as many can be found in a cupful of sea water. A square centimeter of skin (about the size of a fingernail) has in excess of 100,000 organisms. Your intestines are home to billions of these creatures. They occupy everything you touch, taste, smell, and see. They can be found in the air you breathe, the water you drink, and the food you eat. In fact, your entire exterior is made up of one-celled organisms and dying skin cells.

These microorganisms are far from mere building blocks, as once perceived. They are extremely diverse. Most are very functional self-contained units, and often self-reliant. Like tiny, subvisible animals, they have their own version of arms, legs, eyes, skeletal arrangements, immune systems, and command centers. They are designed to fend for themselves, and some clearly have a means of communication.

If one were to assume one-celled organisms were part of the evolutionary progression, then one needs to retreat to the previous era and ask, how did nature make the jump from a collection of loose chemicals to an organism that can survive and reproduce? This arrangement requires a huge number of simultaneous changes. One cannot have an enzyme-driven digestive system in any living species without a way to make these caustic or effective chemicals, a means to safely store them and make new ones, a controlled manner to release them, and a way to terminate their functions. Not at all simple. Impossible in the evolutionary sense.

VIRUSES

Life in the submicrobial world belongs to viruses, whose name is derived from the the Latin word for "poisonous slime." These are complex organisms that, until very recently, were way too small to be seen by any microscope. The vast majority are not poisonous. A million or more can fit on the tip of a needle, billions can be found in every pinch of soil, and trillions live in every mouthful of sea or lake water. They travel about by wind and water currents, inside and outside many different hosts, on keyboards, elevator buttons, banisters, and doorknobs; in blood, semen, street drugs, discharges, stool, urine, contaminated food, and water; and by handshakes, coughs, sharing personal items, kisses, intercourse, and sneezes. Any surface can be their home, for variable lengths of time, under virtually any conditions.

Viruses are literally everywhere, and it seems likely they have helped shape life on Earth since its beginning. Their predecessors are unknown, however, and they may also represent the biggest collection of missing links of all. Every type of virus would have needed millions of chemicals in different combinations and varied shapes that somehow successively built upon themselves. There is also the possibility that they broke free from already living beings—renegade cell parts. No one knows how viruses fit into the theory of evolution, but their overwhelming presence, seeming ancient age, and incredible impact demands an explanation from evolutionists.

For the most part, viruses are a much simpler and smaller form of life than bacteria. They are probably alive, although this is debated by scientists. So far, 4000 different types, along with scores of subtypes, most ranging from 10 to 400 nanometers, have been identified; the actual number of different species may eventually reach the millions. Very recently Dr. Bernard La Scola discovered the unusually large *mimivirus* at the bottom of an old water tower. It is as large as a bacteria, contains 1000 genes with 1.3 million genetic letters, and attacks amoeba, where it resides and reproduces. Some scientists say the mimivirus blurs the beginning of life and viruses should be placed at the base of Darwin's tree of life. Some think this somehow proves evolution, but no one has ever shown a virus mutating into another species of microorganism.

Viruses are by far the most common organism on this planet, and altogether they easily outnumber all other living entities combined. According to Mariso Pedullo, a researcher at the University of Pittsburgh, if viruses were beetles, we would be "buried miles deep" in insects. They can selectively infect bacteria, fish, plants, trees, or animals, in any environment, virtually any time. They can be helpful, a hindrance, benign, or extremely lethal. Or any combination.

Although the purposes, if indeed there are purposes, of most viruses remain unclear, some of the *bacteriophage* (eaters of bacteria) viruses may be keeping us all alive and well. Quintillions-plus live in the sea, and many act like nature's chlorine. Studies show they kill at least 40 percent of bacteria along our seashores; without them our seas would quickly become murky and foul. They also help out by killing huge populations of bacteria that, in turn, are major contributors to carbon dioxide and the greenhouse effect. Are these extremely complex genetic accidents, or an act of Design?

Bad News

The news on viruses is not always good. In humans, certain bacteriophage viruses, living inside diphtheria bacteria, actually make the disease happen. A similar worsening of virulence is true for cholera, a severe type of dysentery that kills thousands each year in developing countries. Another group of bacteriophages will attach to the chromosomes within the streptococcus bacteria and change its method of operation from causing a simple sore ("strep") throat to rheumatic fever, a much more serious heart and joint disease. There's a type of intestinal bacteria that causes a mild infection in humans but turns lethal if an antibiotic is prescribed. As the bacteria dies from the medication, dormant viruses from within are suddenly released.

There is also a wide spectrum of illnesses that are directly caused by viruses, ranging from the common cold, fever blisters, and cruise-ship gastroenteritis (rotovirus) to smallpox, encephalitis, West Nile fever, and SARS. Most viral illnesses cause mild symptoms—a cough, a few loose bowel movements, a rash, a mild fever, or some aches, but some have taken major tolls. A hemorrhagic virus may have destroyed the Aztec nation in the 1500s, not Hernando Cortés. The influenza epidemic of 1918 killed 20 million people worldwide.

Polio killed and maimed millions before the advent of the Salk and Sabin vaccines. The HIV virus has killed millions and may take the largest toll yet. And there are other impending worries around, like avian flu and other viruses that might jump species.

▪▪ AVIAN VIRUS ▪▪

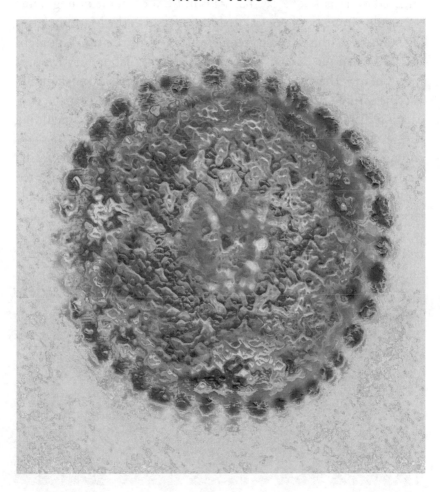

Similar to the pandemic of 1918, a deadly influenza epidemic could be caused by this virus also.

© *James Cavallini / Photo Researchers, Inc.*[4]

Are devastating viral illnesses like smallpox (or any bad outcome) an argument against Intelligent Design? Some Darwinists think so, saying a benevolent Designer would never inflict smallpox on his own creation, or that an Intelligent Designer would not make such "god-awful" mistakes. But there's a flip side. What if humans are accidental hosts—victims—like the surfboarder who is mistaken for a seal and attacked by a shark, or a car that stalls in front of an oncoming train?

Could viruses be biological weapons of a sort? The Marburg virus, also known as the African green monkey virus, became apparent in 1967 when the disease was contracted by 37 laboratory workers in Germany. They were working with monkey cells to make polio vaccines. This virus and its close relative Ebola virus can cause a devastating disease in man. Victims bleed from every orifice including their eyes. No one seems to know how it spreads to monkeys, perhaps through birds or rodents, but hunters seem to contract it by eating bush meat. Villagers contract it by coming into contact with infected bodily fluids. One unlucky physician died when a patient accidentally spat blood on him. The question comes up, are these viruses mutated genetic material gone awry, or some predator-control device from certain jungle dwellers suddenly set loose by our incursions?

▪▪ EBOLA VIRUS ▪▪

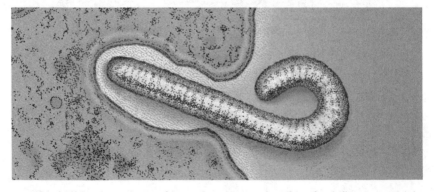

This highly contagious African virus causes an often-fatal illness. Its origin is an enigma.

© Chris Bjornberg / Photo Researchers, Inc.[5]

The rabies virus from the bite of a skunk or a bat might act the same. The carriers don't contract the disease, but their bites can kill off their enemies. The hantavirus found in rodent droppings in Arizona is another killer of man. Did yellow fever accidentally or on purpose come out of the Panama jungle to kill our canal workers? Far-fetched? Maybe, but there are numerous examples of nonviral biological weapons in nature, such as the spit from a poison dart frog, the sting of a man-of-war, and the venom from a cobra. Select colonies of ants will take up residence in certain plants and, in exchange for nectar and a home, will swarm to defend the plant from all intruders, including other insects, mammals, and competing plants. There are certain wasps that aggressively protect bird nests. Parasitoid wasps purposefully sting certain caterpillars, but instead of venom, the sting delivers their eggs plus a batch of polydnaviruses that will knock out the caterpillar's defense mechanisms. The caterpillar will go about its business for about ten days, slowly dying as it is eaten from the inside by growing larvae. The derivation of this virus family seems to be improbable. It can be found only in the ovaries of these wasps, and without this breed of insects, it could not reproduce.

Submicrobial Weaponry

The bacteriophage virus puts out landing pods like the lunar modules, locks in place, and injects its DNA or RNA cargo like a loaded syringe with a needle. Once this cargo has forced the bacteria to make hundreds to thousands of viral particles, they suddenly explode out of the cell, killing it in the process. The Ebola virus infects human cells that line the blood vessels; they swell with increasing viral particles until they explode, causing the victim to hemorrhage throughout their body. This disease can be 90 percent fatal. A very effective biological weapon?

Studying Viruses

To study viruses one needs an electron microscope or certain chemical replication techniques. They come in many shapes including spirals, twisted cords, spheres, and geometric chambers. Bacteriophage viruses often look like microscopic lunar modules, landing and taking off from a cell's surface like the moon, but their design is much more complex than anything man has ever sent into space. Their cargo, sometimes called a command center within a genetic delivery van, is a DNA or RNA blueprint that, upon entering the host's cells, takes over the controls. In some instances the cargo may lie dormant for a while, called lysogeny, and then break out at a very inopportune time for the host. Shingles, or adult chicken pox, is a classic example.

Other viruses merely make use of the host's cells to propagate their own and, possibly accidentally, make the host ill. They inject a nuclear package, commandeer all functions, and begin making clones. This process has several sequential steps that must happen in a definite order and in the correct way, starting with the proper matchup on the cell's surface, traveling to the chromosomes, connecting in a way to stop all other processes, initiating production of specific proteins not seen in these cells beforehand for the virus's external envelope, and then the producing of new DNA or RNA packages inside the correct envelopes. Lastly, they escape by either breaking the cell apart or budding from the cell's surface. Like Dr. Michael Behe's mousetrap analogy of irreducible complexity, this cannot happen unless all the parts are present at the same time and properly linked together. Try to make use of a mousetrap missing any one piece.

Every strain of virus knows what host to attack and which cells are vulnerable or what cellular receptors will work. If it's a virus that normally attacks birds, it will skip over reptiles. If it attacks muscle tissue, it will most likely pass by brain, lung, and kidney cells. Plant viruses will only attack plants, and sometimes it has to be a very specific plant. Different influenza viruses can selectively attack certain mammals and not others. Despite being considered "nonliving" entities by some experts, they have the uncanny ability to mutate (change) like other microorganisms to accomplish their objectives.

Like all living beings, viruses are geared for self-perpetuation. There are no reports of lone chemicals that have produced offspring, whereas viruses do so by the millions. They have complex specific goals and they go about them in very specific ways. They are a very big part of life.

Virus Theory

In Darwin's day, diseases came from bad humors, toxic vapors, and sinful behavior; cures were attempted with good humors, other vapors, and penitence. Viruses were first mentioned in 1898, nearly 40 years after the publication of *The Origin of Species,* by Martinus Beljerinck, a Dutch botanist. But it would take decades before true proof of their presence could be found. The evidence is still being collected.

Throughout the years, supporters of the theory of evolution have chosen to ignore viruses. Dr. Stephen Gould, in *The Book of Life,* allotted them only a single paragraph (out of 250 pages). It begins, "There is one other problematic group, the viruses, which are particularly hard to define." Dr. Roger Lewin's *The Thread of Life: The Smithsonian Looks at Evolution* does not have virus listed in its glossary. In contrast, Dr. Scott Freeman's *Biological Sciences* textbook has a very comprehensive chapter on viruses. In it, he says, "But currently, there is no widely accepted view where viruses came from."

Viruses cannot become fossils or be dated. One evolution theory suggests that they were tiny, runaway, mutated segments of an animal's genes that returned to wreak havoc. One might liken that to a pet dog running away with the house key, mating with a mongrel, and then, several generations later, all of the descendants gaining easy access with that same key, making scores more puppies, and then, as they depart the premises, tearing the place apart.

Another theory argues viruses might be nature's way of communication that went awry. Perhaps ancient cells sent genetic messages back and forth, and then these pre-viruses, altered by external forces, went to wrong hosts and did all the wrong things. We make use of that messaging capability in modern medicine by using altered viruses to treat genetic diseases.

A third idea suggests bacteria were engulfed (eaten) by larger cells, million of years ago, then degenerated inside their predators, reformulated themselves, and escaped as viruses. They cannot survive on their own, meaning to some they are not alive (but tapeworms need hosts and some orchids need trees). All of life is geared toward self-replication, and viruses clearly have that same driving force. A virus may be the ultimate selfish gene.

How they could have evolved remains in the improbable category.

■ ■ ■ ■

The world of microscopic life is a relatively new arena of scientific study. Every discovery leads to many more questions, such as how this could have come about, and even why. Much like us, these invisible beings make use of complex systems every second of their life to survive. Darwin's followers have yet to adequately explain the origin of any of these species. Actually, their silence on the matter is quite noticeable.

PART THREE
IMPROBABLE
NATURAL DESIGNS

A design must be considered improbable if it is highly functional and durable yet too complex to have come about spontaneously or by intermediate steps. Think of the subway system in any large metropolitan area. Could the combination of tracks, stations, tunnels, signs, vending machines, stairwells, lighting, trains, billboards, ticket booths, turnstiles, benches, platforms, security measures, and restrooms have happened all at once or did it come about by stages? If these commuter systems were to follow the tenets of the theory of evolution, the tracks going off in every direction might be called links and the stations called species. How does one get from station to station without a tunnel, train, and tracks? In the theory of evolution, these kinds of intermediaries are abundantly missing.

■ ■ ■ ■ ■

The gecko lizard can easily walk along, up, and down any wall, and across any ceiling, without falling. Electron microscopy has revealed that each lizard has about 500 million suction cups on its toes; each is about .0000008 of an inch wide. Their feet are also formed at a specific angle so they can easily peel off different cups yet remain secure. These suction devices are also self-cleaning. Imagine a dangling ancient lizard crying out for help because it had too loose of a grip. There are no predecessors known.

Velvet worms are thought to be descendants of insects, but the evidence for this is scanty; they look a lot like worms, and they have remained unchanged for millions of years. They live along fallen leaves in tropical forests and have two nozzles, one on each side of their head, which can fire off a very quickly drying glue at their prey. These two sprays crisscross back and forth, as if lassoing the victim. Once the victim is securely ensnared, the worm bites a hole in its body, injects digestive juices, and then slurps up the dissolving victim. Curiously, this glue does not dry within the worm's body, and its digestive juices are well contained. Imagine the difficulty if the intermediate glue dried within the velvet worm, clogging the nozzles, or dried too slowly, allowing the victim to get away before becoming ensnared.

The desert-dwelling chuckwalla lizard maintains its internal temperatures by putting on a dark skin in the morning to absorb heat and then changing to beige later to reflect heat. To compensate for limited water resources, it uses a desalination (desalting) organ in its nose. Much like the iguanas in the Galápagos Islands, it sneezes out salt crystals.

The tongue of a chameleon is launched like a catapult. A combination of slippery sheaths and accelerator muscles can send the tongue shooting off at speeds faster than the eye can see. Special cameras have placed the acceleration at 50G, five times the pressure that causes fighter pilots to black out. Its aim is remarkably precise, easily catching moving insects with a sticky suction cup at the tip of the tongue.

A tropical fish called *Anableps dowi* has four eyes, which look much like two large eyes. There are no clear-cut predecessors. It has two eyes that look above the water and adjust to the brighter light, and two eyes that study the aquatic arena below for predators and separately adjust for the darker light.

The wombat has an upside-down pouch. Scientists presume, and it makes sense, that position prevents dirt from entering the pouch when the wombat is digging in the ground. Could there have been transitional species with pouches situated sideways, or did the first wombats have to scoop dirt out of their pouches every day?

9. MOTION DESIGNS

"The human foot is a masterpiece of engineering and a work of art."

—LEONARDO DA VINCI

It's obvious that movement from one place to another is critical for life to exist. We all need to go somewhere to get food or have it come to us, escape predators, seek out mates, and locate shelter. Getting about seems so simple, like jumping from one lily pad to another, but it is far from it. All muscles need daily exercise or they will wither away; they also need bones to secure them and joints for proper mechanics. Muscle groups typically come paired so that motions like pushing and pulling, lifting or lowering, rotating right and left, grabbing and releasing, and opening and closing can be controlled. There has to be smooth, yet graded, balance. Imagine our handwriting if we all had shaky hands. And would you allow your eyes to be operated on?

Muscle cells are arranged in a purposeful, linear manner. This allows huge groups of them to move in the same direction, at the same speed and with the same effort, in unison. To accomplish their work, muscles need constant nutritional support plus the appropriate concentrations of oxygen for the level of activity, a means to eliminate metabolic products (or else be poisoned), an overseeing mechanism to uniformly control work units, and a method to repair injuries. There could not have been biceps without triceps or hamstrings without quadriceps. The fossil record does not indicate that there were species who had biceps without triceps, quadriceps without hamstrings, or muscles that pushed the tongue out without opposing ones to pull it back in. These functions must either have arrived together, or the record is missing quite a few nonfunctional links.

Life moves about in many varied ways. Most microorganisms take advantage of water or airflow; a few float in the air or surf sneezes; and others can move on their own with whiplike tails, wiggling cilia, cellular crawling, or undulations. The tiniest forms of life are not limited by gravity as we are; but few of us will be blown to Kansas when we were counting on a trip to San Diego. Some micro- and macrospecies hitch a ride inside hosts, such as the bacteria that cause Montezuma's revenge, tapeworms in pigs, and hepatitis viruses in livers. The gypsy moth has buoyant hairs that allow it to ride the winds from continent to continent. Forty different species of hummingbird mites hitch rides in the nostrils of hummingbirds. Since the bird doesn't linger long, they have to be incredibly quick. Carry-on luggage only, please.

Migrating birds make use of air streams; migrating fish use ocean currents. Seeds travel inside birds; pollen travels on the outside of insects. Flowers follow the sun across the sky; the leaves on trees reach up to the sun. Certain mollusks harbor algae to make them food. We all have millions of miniature living beings moving about on our skin, in our eyebrows, and even inside our mouths, nostrils, intestines, and urogenital tracts. For the most part, that's a good thing. Millions also live in our bed pillows. Don't look too closely.

IN THE WATER

Moving across or through water comes in many styles. The dolphin and whale swim with their tail swinging up and down, the opposite of fish tails. Where are the intermediates? Land mammals, their presumed ancestors, mostly move their tails up to defecate or mate. The tubercles which cause scalloped flippers on humpback whales allow them to swim in tighter circles for hunting and decrease drag by 32 percent. A typical fish has unique muscles for diving, changing directions, remaining stationary, and accelerating, fins for rudders, swim bladders to maintain or change buoyancy, and an aeronautical body design.

A paramecium covered with cilia (propelling hairs) swims many times its body length per second. On a human level, that would far exceed the best Olympic swimmer, completing one pool length in ten seconds or less. Cilia only work for the smallest species. If a shark were covered with cilia, the drag would keep it from getting any food. Sleek body shapes and smooth exteriors rule most underwater locomotion, but there are many striking exceptions that challenge evolutionary explanations.

Jet propulsion has "evolved" in many unrelated species. The basic mechanism is expulsion of a liquid out one end to send the animal going in the other way. It usually involves a complex musculature system suddenly squeezing a bag full of fluid. This is the same mechanism we use to move our food from our stomach to our duodenum and expel our urine. Octopi, jellyfish, squid, certain fish, scallops, and cuttlefish travel by jet propulsion. A dragonfly larva accelerates by squirting water out its anus.

IN THE AIR

Flying is another interesting means of locomotion. We live in a sea of air, and our birds are analogous to fish. They both have weight limits, aeronautical designs, and power sources. Many are camouflaged to match their surroundings; many can catch their meals in flight. Symmetry is also extremely important. Not too many birds fly with a single wing.

Every detail of a bird's anatomy is geared for efficient flight. Their bones are hollow and flexible, their wings are structured for easy liftoff and minimal drag, their lungs have additional air sacs throughout their body to increase oxygen uptake. Most birds have the ability to glide or soar, capitalizing on air currents and lessening the energy drain. Some fly in a V-formation to lessen drag. No one knows how they make synchronous changes in direction. Seabirds

Look Out Below!

The Wallace tree frog of Malaysia glides as far horizontally as it does vertically using webbed feet. A flying lizard called a draco has a flattened body and wing like appendages; it can glide 25 feet. There are 40 species of flying fish. The California flying fish shoots out of the water's surface like a torpedo and then opens its fins to glide. Typically, they travel three feet or so, but they've been clocked at speeds of 19 mph and have covered as far as 591 feet. Some can do successive jumps as if flying off the surface. And, there are a few varieties of flying snakes. The ribbon-shaped, golden tree snake of Southeast Asia propels itself off of tree-tops and glides downward for at least 30 feet.

use ground effect, meaning if they are closer to the ground or ocean surface than the width of their wing span, drag is also lessened. Many can catch a meal in flight, which requires unusual timing.

Although there are a few fossils of reptile-like animals with scattered feathers, the chasm between them and modern birds is extremely wide. These structures are made of keratin, the same material in nails and hair. Similar to but fancier than Velcro, they are zipped together by thousands of tiny, interlocking hooks. Feathers are major insulators; if damaged they can be regenerated. Different kinds of feathers grow from different parts of a bird's body, such as those for downy use or flying. Bird wings are more durable than bat wings, which depend on a skin appendage called a patagium. Birds molt two or three times a year at specific, coordinated times, perfectly replacing the older feathers.

Many different species have independently "evolved" the ability to fly, yet this unique function requires much more than a single genetic mutation or a species merely changing from a jumping mode to airborne status.

According to author Jerry Davis in *It's Raining Frogs and Fishes,* "Insect wings are among the engineering marvels of the world. They have evolved into complex structures of incredible strength, flexibility and subtlety." Insects don't glide but flap their wings, and they instinctively know how to change lift and adjust speeds. Their wings are built of longitudinal pleats and have a curvature that reverses with each up and down stroke. They can flap a few hundred times a second and move them several meters per second.

The idea of helicopters comes from watching dragonflies, which are the only insects that can fly backward. Their predecessors were quite similar except closer to an eagle's size. Prior to that is unclear.

■ ■ ■ ■ ■

Motion design is the ultimate choreography. Whether the activity occurs along the ground, in the air, or through the water, billions of muscle, nerve, blood, and bone cells are coordinated to make each part of an animal's body move in exceedingly smooth and select ways that suit them and their survival. A fish navigating a riverbed, a bat flying between trees, and even you turning this page are not consequences of chance mutations or slow evolutionary transitions.

10. STRUCTURE DESIGNS

"To the artist there is never
anything ugly in nature."

—AUGUSTE RODIN

When it comes to citing examples of purposeful design, nearly every author likes to point out the hen's egg. It's really quite remarkable. Despite having a shell that is a mere 0.35 mm thick, they don't break when a parent sits on them. According to Dr. Knut Schmidt-Nielsen,

> A bird egg is a mechanical structure strong enough to hold a chick securely during development, yet weak enough to break out of. The shell must let oxygen in and carbon dioxide out, yet be sufficiently impermeable to water to keep the contents from drying out.

Under microscopy, one can see the shell is a foamlike structure that resists cracking. Gases and water pass though 10,000 pores that average 17 micrometers in diameter. Ultimately, 6 liters of oxygen will have been taken in and 4.5 liters of carbon dioxide given off. The yolk is its food. All life support systems are self-contained, like a space shuttle.

All hen's eggs are ready to hatch on the twenty-first day. Every day is precisely preprogrammed. The heart starts beating on the sixth day. On the nineteenth day the embryo uses its egg tooth to puncture the air sac (beneath the flat end) and then takes two days to crack through the shell.

■ ■ ▓ ▓ ▓

The structures of bones, exoskeletons, and shells are engineered in very specific ways for support, protection, and locomotion. The back legs of deer are set at an angle that allows them to make instant leaps to safety. The bones in bird legs, relatively speaking, are heavier than walking animals to handle the severe impact of landing. The bony structure of fins or wings, although remotely similar to our extremities, differ enough to do what needs to be done. The whale's pelvis supports pelvic organs rather than legs. The spider walks on multiple flexed legs that work like a hydraulic system.

The right structure or bone size, shape, and strength seems to be found in the right places, at the right angles, and with the right fit—every time. Note that Nature does all this without using a speck of metal. There are no bolts, nuts, screws, or I-beams. Everywhere one looks, one can see that Nature has found an equally good or better way. A strand of steel the diameter of spider silk would be one fifth as strong. The strength of a mollusk's shell exceeds our best ceramics. The way a glass might crack is unheard of in Nature.

We use composites like concrete, which is a mixture of sand, gravel, cement, and water, to add strength to many of our structures, but again, milligram for milligram, we can't compete with Nature's concretes. They are stronger and more durable, and they take hold faster. There isn't time to put up a sign saying, *Recently Poured Snail Shell.*

The conch shell may only be 1/8th inch thick, but it is extremely crack-resistant. It is made up of a composite of crisscrossing, perpendicular rods of aragonite, which are also made up of rods, and 1 percent protein glue. It can also, unlike our buildings, repair itself. The external skeleton of a starfish is loaded with strategically placed crystals and microscopic holes, some smaller than 1/50th of an inch, that prevent a crack from spreading. A break should stop at the first hole. Wood, likewise, is stronger than its individual components.

The fossil records should be loaded with intermediate shells and exoskeletons. It is not.

11. CHEMICAL DESIGNS

"LAB RULES:
1. First draw your curves,
then plot your data.
2. If you can't get the answer
in the usual manner, start at the
answer and derive the question."

—ANONYMOUS

The DuPont-coined phrase "Better Living Through Chemistry" can readily be applied to all living organisms. We all depend on an uncountable number of chemical reactions. Just look at the six billion nucleotide bases that make up human chromosomes. They are found in each of our ten-trillion-plus cells. Then, add in the billions of proteins that work as chemical on-off switches, enzymes, and messengers. The structure of many of these proteins is more convoluted than a skein of wool, yet every component has to be in an exact position, bent correctly, and have the right electrical charge.

DuPont later changed their advertising phrase to "Better Living Through the Miracles of Science." Below are a few of the relatively simple chemical miracles.

■ ■ ■ ■ ■

Hemoglobin and hemocyanin are respiratory proteins that lie within the red blood cells and are responsible for carrying oxygen to other parts of the body. They increase the oxygen-carrying capacity of serum by 100 times and drastically reduce the work of the heart. Without this protein, our hearts could not keep up with our needs; we literally could not exist. Most of the hemoglobins found in animals and plants contain iron, copper, chromium, zinc, and even tin or nickel. For unexplained reasons, only sea squirts use vanadium. This lacks an evolutionary explanation.

Most higher vertebrates have the same concentration of hemoglobin, but there are built-in mechanisms to increase the levels if the animal is a deep-diver or high-flyer where oxygen levels are diminished. Insects don't need hemoglobin; they make use of gas diffusion laws and absorb oxygen from tubules that line their exoskeleton and extend throughout the body. Microorganisms, because of their small size, can make use of similar diffusion laws.

TO GLUE OR NOT TO GLUE?

The adhesive used by barnacles is among the strongest in the world. It is reported that a layer merely 3/10,000 of an inch thick can support a weight of 7000 pounds. This relative of the shrimp and crab glues its head down and keeps its feet up to catch the next meal. Its adhesive sets in water at any temperature and will not dissolve in most acids, bases, and solvents. Fossil records suggest it has been used by barnacles unchanged for 400 million years. Nothing seems to be known about its intermediates before that.

Mussels have a similar glue, which sets underwater and has enormous strength. It takes about five minutes for the mussel to create a "dab" of this glue beneath its foot on a piling or rock. Twenty dabs will do it, and the job can be completed overnight. Imagine the consternation of intermediate species when they secreted what they thought was glue, but kept being washed away by the waves. Or the species that couldn't store their glue and found their bivalves stuck together.

Adhesion is a basic necessity of life. Microorganisms chemically adhere in biofilms to a variety of surfaces, or else they would be repeatedly blown or washed away. Pollen must stick to the stigma during fertilization. Food must stick to a lizard's tongue; ants must stick to an anteater's tongue. Cells have a complex method of adhesion, allowing them to interact with neighbor cells and maintain structures. Without the ability of cells to adhere to each other in a designated way, one's liver might be an amorphous bag of liver cells.

■ ■ ■ ■ ■

Darwin didn't have a clue about the life-sustaining chemical reactions that occur in our bodies or indeed in any animal's body. His view was very superficial, much like that of a person who buys a car based on the paint job only. Billions of chemical reactions happen on a millisecond-by-millisecond basis in all living organisms. Nearly every preceding step to every reaction—and in most cases there are hundreds of steps—is a missing link. Billions of defined links are missing in every cell.

12. PLANT DESIGNS

"The creation of a thousand
forests is in one acorn."

— RALPH WALDO EMERSON

In many ways the interaction between the animal kingdom and the plant kingdom is like a game of catch. We toss out carbon dioxide molecules (from our lungs); plants catch them (with their leaves) and turn them into oxygen molecules and then toss them back. This exchange may have been going on for millions of years and it is vital to the survival of nearly every living entity on the planet.

No one truly knows how this interaction arose. The theory of evolution suggests that algae somehow arose from the primordial sea and then evolved into underwater plants, which eventually came ashore as flat plants to see more of the world or escape predators, changed to upright plants to see more of the sky, and then changed to wooded plants to see even more of the sky. Somehow they extracted carbon dioxide from a dismal ancient atmosphere that lacked oxygen and started producing oxygen for unclear reasons even though there were no animals around who used it; and the oxygen eventually plateaued at an atmospheric concentration of 21 percent. Animal life would require this level. This scenario through the millennia combines an incredible collection of coincidences...perhaps a miraculous collection. Scores of intermediate steps (links) are missing all along the line. Changing minestrone soup into garlic bread with a change of atmosphere would be easier.

The chemical reactions that every leaf uses to convert carbon dioxide back to oxygen can be expressed rather simply: add six molecules of water to six molecules of carbon dioxide, place in the sunlight (amount varies with each plant), and you will soon have one molecule of sugar (for the plant and others) and six molecules of oxygen (for the animals). But this is far from simple. The enzymes, the mechanisms, the transport, the control and storage could easily take a chapter each. By the time science is done, each step will probably require a book.

The plant's side of this interaction requires the presence of a pigment called chlorophyll, which is found inside microscopic pea-shaped green organelles within each cell of every leaf. Some scientists think they might once have been green microorganisms that were trapped and then passed on, but that's only speculation—and if so, a rather striking combination of accidents. Notably, chloroplasts are found at the top of every plant or are spread out along branches and limbs so that they can capture the most sunlight. A plant evolving without chloroplasts is like a book without pages. They had to have arrived together.

These chemical factories make use of all wavelengths of visible light except green. Why only green is reflected is not known, but one could argue that it was designed to help us identify plant life. Imagine how it would be if plants absorbed all wavelengths and we had black trees, black broccoli, and black lettuce.

■ ■ ■ ■ ■

It doesn't take much of a close look to appreciate the complexity and intricacy of any plant's design. Take the cuticle or waxy surface on every leaf that prevents the unnecessary loss of water or gases. This is quite different than their "predecessors" from the sea and it presents an interesting conundrum. Did the first attempted landings of plants result in straw because they lacked this protection, or did underwater plants develop a cuticle when they didn't need it?

The water for the sustenance of life is procured from the root system and the air through very complex mechanisms, especially in tall trees or any foliage in arid climates. Every leaf is dotted with microscopic mouth-shaped openings, called *stomata,* which are lined by two guard cells. When the plant is low on water, they become soft and close the opening to retain water; when the plant is well hydrated, they stiffen and thereby open to allow evaporation. They also allow oxygen in and carbon dioxide out.

Cacti expand and shrink like an accordion based on water content, and Australian acacia trees are shaped like upside-down umbrellas to catch the scanty rainfall.

Leaves have many other interesting designs as well. They will furrow or roll up as the wind intensifies; the greater the wind speed, the tighter the cone. They also shift like a weather vane, lessening the drag and the chance of being broken off. As winter comes and the chances of maintaining good health diminish, trees automatically stop making chlorophyll. Carotenoid pigments take over, which change leaf colors to the autumn reds, yellows, and oranges. A tree hormone causes a layer of cells at the base of each leaf to die and seal the base. When the process is complete, the leaf falls away.

And the tree hunkers down for the season.

The upright posture of plants is a striking design that falls short of a clear explanation. The pat answer is that prehistoric flat plants decided to go vertical to compete for more sun. But where did this need to compete arise? And how could a limp ground hugger accidentally develop systems to support excessive weight—maybe tons of wood—root systems to support the weight, transport systems to move the water and nutrients up, and defense mechanisms against weather and pests? Much of it had to be there at the same time. An analogy that I used in my previous book readily applies. The spontaneous appearance of an upright plant would be like taking a walk from New York City to Los Angeles and then pointing out how easy it was because your first step took you to Cleveland and the second one to Chicago.

Another Incredible Evolutionary Conundrum

The fig and the fig wasp have a fascinating one-to-one relationship; neither species can live without the other and both depend on critical timing. Certain fig tree species can only be pollinated by a particular fig wasp species that lives within the fruit; they, in turn, can only feed in the fig's ovary. This fruit is unique in that it is hollow and contains hundreds of its flowers of both sexes inside. Female flowers mature first.

When the fig is ready for pollination it gives out a scent that attracts a particular female wasp which is usually no larger than a tiny ant. She enters through a minute opening in the fig that is so tight that she usually breaks off her wings and antennae. As she is pollinating all of the flowers inside, she also deposits an egg in each of the short-stemmed flowers. Because she cannot reach the ovary of the long-stemmed flowers to deposit an egg, they will form seeds. When the offspring mature, this plant's pollen is ready for transport. The male offspring, who is blind and wingless, gnaws his way out of his part of the ovary, then gnaws his way to the

PLANT DESIGN ODDITIES

When we think of plants or trees, we generally assume they are the same temperature as the environment and primarily subsist on the nutrients either procured from their surroundings or self-manufactured. There are, however, some very odd exceptions that challenge the theory of evolution.

According to an article by Susan Milius, several hundred types of plants across ten families can generate and sometimes maintain heat like warm-blooded animals, but without blood. Specific male cells keep reproductive parts warmer than their surroundings; some plants, like the eastern skunk cabbage, can melt the snow around them.

The Mediterranean dead-horse arum is a good example. This is a pink-colored flower whose spath (a poker in the center of the flower) can generate heat as fast as the muscles in the wings of birds. The warmth helps spread a foul dead-carcass smell that attracts female blowflies who, in turn, flock there to lay their eggs. They bring pollen from other arums, pollinate these female organs, and then are trapped for a day or so by temporary spines. During this programmed time period, they will pick up the slower-maturing male's pollen and carry it to the next fake, smelly carcass.

female and mates with her, then gnaws his way out of the fig entirely and commits *hari-kari*, by falling or jumping out of the hole. The new female, who happens to have wings, follows him out attracting some new pollen dust as she goes and flies away to repeat the cycle.

Insect-eating plants are another hard variation in evolution to explain. Although most people might think they are rare, there are 600 carnivorous species and sub-species in eight different flowering families. It appears as if the need to eat insects is present as a back-up option to get protein if the soil is poor in nitrogen and phosphorus. None of these plants seem to turn down an opportunity to eat a good fly sushi and, although they lack the same neurological systems and muscles for movements typically possessed by animals, some can attack their victims and some have biological weapons. All have the capability of digesting their victims.

The Venus flytrap is one of the best known carnivorous plants. Colorful flowers attract potential prey, and once an insect lands, exquisitely sensitive hair cells send an electrical message to hinge cells located along the spine. They cause the two halves to close instantly, trapping the victim in a cagelike space where it dies—and as it decays, the plant absorbs the nutrients. Notably, it has a mechanism built in to distinguish animate from inanimate particles and will not close on a tiny pebble unless it is moving.

The pitcher plant attracts insects by aromatic secretions along the surface of a treacherous pitcher. The plant's design is such that the insects will slide down the waxy walls into a pool of water and enzymes, never to escape. The sundew plant has sticky hairs on its leaves that will immobilize an insect. Then, when it senses the insect struggling, the leaves pull together and the plant secretes enzymes to digest it.

Assuming plants did not start out as carnivores, and nobody knows precisely what the first plants looked like or how they survived, the change could not have been an easy transition. It's hard to imagine a plant evolving the ability to sense the presence of an insect without the ability to capture it or the ability to trap the next meal without the ability to digest it. Each of these are enormously complex processes and they had to have arrived at the same moment in time. To think otherwise would be illogical.

Interestingly enough, Darwin was fascinated by the Venus flytrap. His experiments showed that feeding meat to some made them healthier than their unfed, soil-dependent siblings. It's not clear how he thought they fit into evolution. Could there have been a cage but no digestive juices?

■■■■■

Not only are plants complex factories that are made up of millions of smaller, interactive factories, but they can also procure very select elements from their environment, accomplish complex jobs, compete in many unusual ways, and defend themselves from microbes, other plants, and even some animals. Could a plant have accidentally learned how to use (and find) very specific microbes along its root structures to retrieve nutrients, or a tree raise tons of water hundreds of feet high? How many mistaken pathways (links) would it have taken a tree before it could make apples (with seeds) from manure, sunlight, and water? One mistake—and that species no longer exists. These kinds of transitional steps (links) have been ignored far too long.

13. NATURE'S LAWS

"At every level of scale, from molecules to ecosystems, we find mathematical patterns in innumerable aspects of life."

—IAN STEWART, **LIFE'S OTHER SECRETS**

Virtually everything around us—every species, and everything we see, hear, do, say, breathe, drink, eat, and feel—is regulated by some natural law. Sounds are perceived in decibels, colors in wavelengths, scents in shapes, and pain in electrical signals. How we walk, run, jump, and touch can be expressed by distances, angles, frequencies, and speed. We all, from the smallest algae to the largest whale, are measurable beings living in a regulated, quantifiable electrical, mechanical, and chemical world.

■ ■ ■ ■ ■

Many laws of physics are incredibly complex, such as the gravitational force, the strong force, electromagnetic force, the weak force, Newton's laws, the laws of thermodynamics, Planck's constant, and Einstein's theories; only physicists think they understand them. Other laws are much more tangible, like measurements of the air we breathe. It has concentration, pressure, humidity, temperature, and volume. You can tell there's a transparent sea of air out there by watching a tornado swirl or, like children do, putting your hand outside a moving car. Our water has predictable freezing and boiling points; and it always flows downhill. Light always travels at 186,282 miles per second. Sound travels at 700 mph. Both radiate out in perfect spheres.

The Earth is spinning at 1000 mph, and the sun, along with the solar system, is moving toward the Virgo galaxies at a speed of 400 miles per second. But one cannot feel it. The solar system rotates around the Milky Way at a definable speed and frequency, as do the planets around the sun and the moon around the Earth. Toss a ball into the air and it decelerates at a calculated rate. Drop anything and it will fall at a specific speed. Every metal has a measurable strength; every gem has a measurable hardness. Shoot a cannonball into the air and it will follow the same trajectory down as it did going up. Gravity impacts us all, but there are rules based on the size of the individual and the planet. A 150-pound man on Earth will weigh 4100 pounds on the sun, 380 pounds on Jupiter, and 25 pounds on the moon. These are universal laws.

There are set atmospheric cycles that follow definite rules as well. All are important to our survival, most are critical. Carbon dioxide goes full circle from volcano eruptions, industrial and auto exhausts, ocean life, and exhaled breath of animals to removal by plants, the weathering of rocks by rainwater and metabolism in the seas.

Seventy percent of the earth's surface is water, and 90 percent of that is ocean. Only 3 percent of the total water is fresh water, and three-quarters of that is frozen at the polar ice caps. In essence, we directly depend on less than 1 percent of all water. Fortunately, water can exist in three major forms. An accident? Heat evaporates it from the oceans to form clouds, it moves over land, cools, and condenses back to water, snow, or ice. It then returns to earth, re-nourishes both plant and animal life, and returns to the sea. How might it be here if water could not make the changes to complete this cycle?

PHYSIOLOGY

Much of our inner body can be described in mathematical terms. Blood pressure, pulse, and temperature can be measured. We burn a specific number of calories per unit of work. We eat and drink

specific volumes, and we burn, sweat, and eliminate comparable volumes. Our skin can sense gradients of temperature changes, variable
pressures, and electrical charges. What we lift, pull, or push comes
in weights, lengths, heights, distances, and types of force. Impulses
travel along nerves at a very specific speed. Blood has a specific
viscosity (thickness). It moves at a controlled rate and its contents
are tightly regulated at specific concentrations. Knees and backs
are designed to support a certain amount of weight. The eyes blink
at a tenth of a second. A rise in antibodies is predictable, stomach
acid is secreted in expected volumes, and hormones do their work
at specific concentrations.

There is a predictable rhythm to each day. Most of us sleep and
wake at nearly the same time, eat at the same time, and have "our
constitutional" at the same time. Some of us get cranky (or nice) at the
same time of the month. As we age we all pass the same milestones:
fetus, newborn, toddler, preteen, adolescent, and adulthood. We
decline in a measurable pattern; we even die by certain numbers.

In many physical ways we are designed to be biorobots, all cut
from the same or similar cookie cutter. But there's that unusual
capability to think and feel. Is it an electrochemical illusion? Do
we just think we think?

Natural laws govern all aspects of our physiology. Body mass and
blood volume in mammals are intricately related. Simply stated, the
bigger the animal, the more blood is needed. Even the heart size is
dependent on body size. No surprise that the whale's heart can be as
big as an SUV. Certain bones are designed to withstand the pressure
of weight-bearing plus the intensified pressures from locomotion,
acceleration, and deceleration. The pressure on a bull elephant's feet
while grazing is nothing compared to the pressures on its soles if it
suddenly charges at a lion. The pressure on a squirrel's legs is much
more intense with that jump from branch to branch than standing
stationary. The bones, joints, tendons, and ligaments have to withstand a wide range and be efficient and functional at all levels.

The body skeleton increases with body mass—bigger, sturdier

bones are needed to carry heavier bodies. According to Professor Knut Schmidt-Nielsen, author of *Scaling*, one of the largest land animals that ever lived was the baluchitherium. It is a presumed relative of the rhinoceros. Based on fossilized foot bones, the adult weighed 30 tons and stood about two-and-a-half times the height of an average man. Schmidt-Nielsen estimates those bones could withstand the pressure of 240 tons.

Metabolic rates seem to go in the reverse. In general, the larger the animal, the slower its metabolism. It's not the size of the animal that counts as much as it is the surface-to-air ratio; smaller animals have a relatively greater body surface than larger ones. That means a smaller animal loses heat more easily and must eat more and work harder to just maintain. A shrew's heart rate is 1000 per minute, whereas an elephant's heart beats 30 times per minute. Life expectancy is essentially the opposite, making one think every species' heart has only so many beats allotted in a lifetime.

The speed at which a fish can swim per second can be calculated from its body length. If one accounts for size, nearly all fish swim at the same relative speed. The beat of the tail correlates with distance moved. A bee flaps its wings every five milliseconds. The spiral of a snail shell is a function of the golden ratio, the Divine proportion, and the golden rectangle. All these are common mathematical formulas.

Plants follow mathematical rules as well. They grow in ways that resist the pull of gravity and unfold in ways that maximize their leaf exposure to the sunlight. Seedlings can be planted upside down, sideways, or flat and they always know which way is up. By accident? Trees raise water from the ground to enormous heights using rules of physics and chemistry.

RATIOS AND SYMMETRY

There's an extremely common yet peculiar preference for certain numbers in nature. One of these is the Fibonacci sequence of numbers, wherein the next number is the sum of the previous two:

▪▪ CONSISTENT RATIOS IN ANATOMY ▪▪

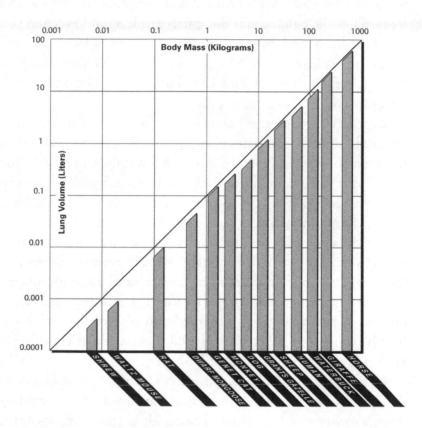

Nearly all anatomical structures and physiological function in all animals follow the same mathematical relationships. The ratios of heart size to body size, internal temperature to metabolism, and bone strength to body weight was determined long ago, and the rules continue to this day.

Illustration by Dana Csakany

1, 1, 2, 3, 5, 8, 13, 21, 34, 55, 89, 144, 233, and so on. This sequence has been discussed for centuries. Many petals, sepals, leaves, and seeds follow the ratio. Count the spirals inside a sunflower and you will most likely find 34 clockwise and 55 counterclockwise ones. It can, on occasion, go to 89 and 144. Pineapples have 8 sloping scales going one direction and 13 going the other. Pine cones will typically have 3, 5, or 8 scales per row.

A geometric constant in nature is symmetry. This means having a balanced form, like both sides of an airplane, or around an axis like a tennis ball or Frisbee. Note the monarch butterfly with its perfectly matching wings or a millipede with synchronous legs. We have two symmetric halves (side to side, not front to top). The starfish has a radial type of symmetry.

Any deviation from the usual design prompts the question, what's wrong with him, her, or it? Symmetry is much more than mere aesthetic appreciation, however. It has definite mechanical advantages. Imagine how a bear would survive if its teeth were misaligned, how a horse would gallop if its legs were randomly placed, or a bird would fly if its wings were different sizes. Did these symmetries evolve? If so, there's a lot of weird fossils still missing.

A classic representation of symmetry can be found in Leonardo da Vinci's Vitruvian Man. His famous model was drawn standing inside a square superimposed on a circle. The square component has his legs together and his arms reaching out, indicating our height equals the distance between our outstretched fingertips (we form a square). The circle component has the arms lifted up about ten degrees with the legs held apart (we also form a circle).

Our lives constantly follow the rules of symmetry. Even in utero the eyes, ears, arms, legs, fins, wings, or flukes arise at the same time and develop in unison. Under normal circumstances there are no unilateral appendages. There is an ongoing coordination in development that we do not fully understand, and there are no hints of any intermediate ways of developing that preceded simultaneous symmetry.

Artists have made use of human symmetry for centuries. One

can find an equilateral triangle between our pupils and the tip of our nose, another from the edges of our mouth to the bridge of our nose, a third from our shoulders to our navel, and a fourth from our navel to our hips. Our left hand is a near-mirror image of our right hand. Imagine how effective our hands would be if the fingers were reversed. Our height is, on average, seven-and-one-half heads tall. Our eyes are normally separated by the width of one eye. The forearm equals the foot size. So does the circumference of one's fist, which is the old-fashioned way of buying socks. The human face is two hands wide. Our nose is in the longitudinal middle of our face; our mouth is halfway between our nose and our chin. The ends of the mouth line up with the pupils. Given a little talent, one can easily draw a face by using a formula and graph paper.

Parts fit together; there are no intermediates that are half Ford and half Chevy. The exact same number of ribs attach in the middle of the chest and the middle of the back. Comparable muscles push and pull. Our front side complements our back side; our top half fits with our bottom half. We naturally fold in the right places to sit in a chair, twist in the right places to look to the side, and flatten out to lie down on a bed. We all come with a natural, calculable center of gravity.

There is a common denominator to the symmetries of life that is based on a mathematical concept called the divine proportion. This ratio is approximately 1.61803 to 1 and appears to be a natural law.

Envision a transacted line whose total length (ABC) compared to the larger segment (AB) is the same as the ratio of the larger segment (AB) to the smaller segment (BC). Any rectangle whose length and width corresponds to this ratio is called a golden rectangle. For unclear reasons these rectangles are more pleasing to the eye than other rectangles. One can see this same shape in everything from the Parthenon to paintings by the old masters to modern billboards and paperback books. Every spiral-shaped shell can be broken down to this rectangle.

■ ■ ■ ■ ■

Natural laws govern our existence. Like a bridge designed by an engineer, most structures in the living world fit into or can be explained by mathematical equations. Did the perfectly suited protective cushion in an elephant's foot come before its hefty torso? Or did they come together? The evidence does not show a long line of crippled elephants breeding until the right cushion happened by mutation. And so it goes with nearly every aspect of every animal and plant.

14. TREASURE HUNT

"Perhaps the most crucial factor driving the search for new medicines from nature is the increasing realization of the incredible diversity (and medical potential) that Mother Nature harbors."

—MARK J. PLOTKIN, PHD, AUTHOR OF MEDICINE QUEST

Are all edible plants, potable liquids, materials for clothing, fuels for keeping warm, raw products to create shelter, and minerals to make metals, cosmetics, and lifesaving medications found in Nature merely a consequence of our ingenuity and good fortune (meaning they aren't found on Mars and Mercury), or are they purposefully designed and hidden for an epoch-long treasure hunt? For example, penicillin and streptomycin, both antibiotics, are normally manufactured by common fungi. After Dr. Fleming discovered penicillin, other researchers learned how to reproduce it. Since World War Two we've made many variants of this lifesaving medicine.

There's an anesthetic that comes from frogskin, a blood thinner taken from leeches, a way to close wounds with the pincers of soldier ants, and a woman's hormone that can be separated from horse urine. Could these findings be the scientific equivalent of the artist who claims there's a statue hidden in a block of granite? Or is this simply the work of a clever human being who finds two sticks, rubs them together, and makes a fire?

Nearly all of our antibiotics and antifungals—and most of our heart medicines, pain-killers, muscle relaxants, anti-inflammatories, anticoagulants, and cancer cures—are either extracted from natural compounds or modified natural derivatives. Many biological gems have been found literally in tree bark, coal fields, backyard dirt, snail slime, flower petals, backyard weeds, oil deposits, and wild roots.

The term *bioprospecting* is sometimes applied to those who hunt the wilds for human benefit and it's become a big business. So is *bioemulating*. This is a term for copying nature's mechanics. Examples include streamlining cars and submarines like dolphin bodies, manufacturing telephone transducers to work like eardrums, making chain saws emulate beetle jaws, and making materials adhere with Velcro, whose design is taken from burrs.

ANCIENT MEDICINES

The use of natural compounds for medicinal reasons is not new. Ancient Egyptians had 850 plant remedies. Among them was the application of a green-blue mold to infections, which might have been an early use of an antibiotic. The Greeks also used mold from their gymnasium walls to treat infections. The Chinese used moldy soybeans, milkmaids in the Middle Ages used moldy bread. The 5000-year-old Iceman who was found in the Italian Alps had fungal medicinal powders in his pouch.

According to May Berenbaum, PhD, an entomologist at the University of Illinois, the Egyptians used honey on wounds three millennia ago. Supposedly, Alexander the Great's body was transported immersed in honey for preservation. Now, with the advent of antibiotic-resistant bacteria, honey therapy is seeing a mild resurgence. It contains natural antibiotics and enzymes that normally protect the hive. It might protect us also.

Opium has been used as a painkiller for nearly 6000 years. Excavations of several Neolithic Swiss villages have uncovered fossilized poppy seeds in close proximity to living quarters. Hippocrates recognized its addictive potential and advised against its use; Napoléon was rumored to have used it to euthanize his wounded soldiers. Curare, which is a plant toxin used by South American Indians to poison their arrows, is also used by anesthesiologists in much smaller doses as a muscle relaxant—not to poison their patients.

Myrrh, which comes from a tree resin, was also used in ancient times as a medication. Recent studies have shown that it has antifungal and antistaphylococcus qualities. The question has been raised by other authors as to whether Joseph and Mary were given myrrh as a fragrance or a medication. Even frankincense has some medicinal benefits.

AMAZING SOURCES

The list of medications derived from nature is enormous and growing. Scientists estimate that there are 125,000 to 750,000 medications yet to be discovered. That's assuming the "human meteor" doesn't destroy Nature first. Nontraditional folks in Western cultures want "natural remedies" whenever possible, without realizing that a great many of the standard prescriptions are derived from natural sources.

Fennel and silphium (now extinct) were used as contraceptives in Roman and Greek times. Aspirin comes from the willow tree, whose bark was tasted by Reverend Edward Stone in 1757. His thinking was that cures could be found nearby illnesses. Digitalis is a traditional folk medicine for heart disease, now used by cardiologists worldwide. It comes from the foxglove flower and is used for congestive heart failure and certain irregularities.

Quinine, which is a major therapy for malaria, comes from the bark of the cinchona tree. This tree was named after the Countess of Chinchon, the wife of a Peruvian viceroy, who was dying of a fever and was saved by a powdered bark from native Indians. Artemisinin, another malaria treatment, comes from Chinese herbal medicines. Atropine for bowel problems comes from the belladonna plant. Taxol for ovarian cancer comes from the yew tree. Menthol comes from the peppermint tree. Cocaine, although illegal, is also an analgesic. It comes from Peruvian peasants, who chew coca leaves and has led to its use as a dental anesthetic. Two chemotherapy agents come from the periwinkle flower. The hugely marketed blood-pressure pill Capoten resulted from studies on the Brazilian viper.

The first plant that was used for medicinal purposes will remain obscure. One might speculate that a desperately ill individual simply tried a leaf or a root, out of blind hope. Or, more likely, someone viewed an ill or wounded animal eating a specific leaf. Indeed, the latter explanation has some basis in fact. The pigweed, which is eaten in India to treat worms, was discovered by practitioners of folk medicine watching wild boars eagerly dig it up and eat it. As it turns out, the weed has definite antihelminthic (worm-killing) capability. The fig and *Aspilia rudis* leaves are eaten by chimpanzees probably for the same reason (to treat worms). It has been shown that young fig leaves have 600 percent more antihelminthic potential than older leaves.

Native societies have commonly used local flora for medicinal needs. According to Mark J. Plotkin, author of *Medicine Quest,* the Chacobo tribe in Bolivia uses 95 percent of the local tree species, the Tembe people of Brazil use 61.3 percent; and the Ka'apoor tribe uses 76.8 percent. Native American shamans along the Amazon used to use a boiled roach tea to settle down cranky children. Of course, this might settle me down too. Ancient Aztecs used at least 150 different medicinal plants.

An herb that is extracted from the berries of the American saw palmetto is recommended by physicians worldwide for possible improved prostate health. It is the same plant that was originally used by native Americans for urinary problems. Supposedly, the palmetto extract shrinks an enlarged prostate and thereby allows the bladder to empty more easily. It also lessens the chances of getting an infection, improves sleep (one does not have to get up so often), and definitely postpones, if not eliminates, the need for surgical intervention.

Many medicines come from the polypeptides and proteins found in snake venom. A toxin from the Asian pit viper may prevent a melanoma from spreading, an Israeli scorpion may limit brain cancer, the Gila monster may stimulate insulin, the Cameroon tarantula may treat neurological diseases, and the Russell pit viper may test for certain arthritic conditions.

The medication AZT used for HIV comes from a fungus called NIM-811. Botox, a nerve poison from the clostridia bacteria, can be used in tiny doses to treat tremors, tics, wrinkles, spastic vocal cords, and maybe migraine headaches. The drug cyclosporin, used to prevent transplant rejections, comes from the fungus tolypocladium. The large family of "statins" prescribed for high cholesterol originally came from a fungus found in the soil. The blood thinner warfarin comes from spoiled sweet clover. It was discovered when a cow herd began hemorrhaging to death.

Calcitonin, which is used for osteoporosis, comes from salmon. ArC for chemotherapy comes from a sponge and Ara-A from the herpes virus. The chemical cantharidin, which we use to burn warts, comes from the female blister beetle. Sunscreen comes from coral. Bee venom has ten active chemicals that may lessen the pain of rheumatoid arthritis, while fire ants have antibiotics in their saliva that they spray over their offspring.

The development of analgesics, or pain relievers, from neurotoxins is another example. A new standout is ziconotide taken from a South Pacific cone snail. According to Mark Plotkin, for their size, they are the deadliest creatures on our planet. Their tongue is covered with syringes loaded with deadly

Vaccines

The smallpox vaccination makes use of a natural phenomenon, that being the body's ability to make antibodies and to recognize a microscopic intruder. The idea of how to protect us from microscopic killers came from Pasteur's observation that women who milked cows were exposed to the cowpox virus and did not contract smallpox. Both viruses are very similar. His subsequent vaccination of others with the cowpox blisters, protected them from smallpox and ultimately saved millions of lives. Specific antibodies were the protection, but he didn't know that then.

Pasteur's discovery led to a host of other valuable vaccines including tetanus, diphtheria, hepatitis A and B, measles, influenza, mumps, rubella, chicken pox, and polio, which have saved enormous amounts of suffering and deaths. Science now understands the immune system much better and there is current research into vaccines for select cancers and Alzheimer's disease.

poison. Each species may have up to 200 different venoms and there are 500 species of cone snails.

LEECHES AND MAGGOTS

Leeches are another interesting medicinal use of natural resources. Nowadays, surgeons utilize them to control swelling and unwanted clots near the reattachment of fingers, noses, toes, and ears. The less engorged the wound becomes, the better the chance of successful healing.

Ancient bloodletting was done for different reasons. Paintings on the tombs of Egyptian pharaohs depict leeches on bodies. The Greeks claimed these creatures helped balance the four major humors of the body. Reportedly, the red-and-white spiral poles outside barber shops reflect the ancient bloody, white bandages that were once hung outside barbers' "shops" as advertisements.

In 1833, France imported 40 million leeches after being convinced by one of Napoléon's former medical officers that they should be used for all types of inflammation. In fact, the man himself was a leech addict. That craze led to a demand that nearly drove the species to extinction.

There are over a hundred different proteins in leech saliva. At least one is an anesthetic that completely blocks the would-be pain of their penetration or bite. Another works as an anticoagulant (blood thinner) that keeps the individual's blood chemicals from setting off a clotting cascade as well as keeping the meal from clotting within their own stomachs. A third type of protein prevents platelets from getting sticky and clotting off the wound in another fashion. All accidents of nature that appear to have arrived together? Quite the coincidence? One might speculate that leech bites without the pain reliever would not have boded well for the species.

The use of blowfly maggots is another resurgent use of an old natural remedy. Flies have been used for wound care by isolated tribes in Central America and Australia for centuries. Officers in Napoléon's army noted that soldiers whose wounds were infested with maggots often did better than those whose wounds weren't. Maggots were also utilized during the Civil War, when officers noticed the same phenomenon.

Flies are one of nature's recyclers and they thrive on dead, putrefying, and dying tissues. If raised sterile, they can incise and debride a ragged, infected wound a thousand percent better than the best surgeon. They destroy harmful bacteria with chemicals in their saliva, sterilize the wound with select aluminum and calcium compounds, and manage to do their work without causing any pain. They also leave smaller scars.

■ ■ ■ ■ ■

There's no way to scientifically determine Purpose or the lack of it when it comes to bioprospecting. An intriguing question remains, however: Why are there so many useful and lifesaving items within our reach? If the Earth were merely a huge collection of dust particles after the big bang, how did it get all these useful products?

PART FOUR
IMPROBABLE NATURAL FUNCTIONS

Picture a hospital functioning without beds, medications, nurses, or doctors. It can't happen. Every piece of this system is needed. Imagine a skyscraper without ventilation or a city without traffic control. In a like manner every living function depends on other, equally complex functions. Most, if not all, are too incredible to have happened by mere survival of the fittest or undirected accidents.

Your body contains 10 to 75 trillion cells that are constantly working to keep you healthy. The 35 billion nerve cells help you think, balance, hear, feel, smell, and see (plus many thousand other functions). The human heart will beat about 3 billion times in an average lifetime and pump close to 50 million gallons of blood, to specific places in specific ways. The human lungs will breathe 8 million times during an average lifetime, basically sampling all the air in a small city and then some. The human kidneys will cleanse over 13 million gallons of blood. The gastrointestinal tract will process over 25 tons of food and defecate four-and-a-half miles of feces (not my measurement). And this is all done simultaneously and automatically for us. Complexity truly isn't the question. The envelope of unthinkable combinations is being pushed.

■■■■■

Although we retain some minor veto power (like holding our breath, taking a laxative, or postponing a meal), the vast majority of physiological functions are self-regulating systems. Your body constantly monitors your oxygen concentration, carbon dioxide levels, blood pressure, heart rate, kidney function, immune status, balance, salt concentrations, internal temperature and controls, hydration status and corrective actions, red and white blood cell production, saliva production, gastric juice production, bowel movements, bile production, fatigue levels, a myriad of hormone levels and their impact, tactile signals and your responses, blood sugar and insulin levels, and sounds, sights, and smells. Should your oxygen levels drop below a safe concentration or your carbon dioxide concentration rise too high, you will automatically breathe faster, deeper, or both. If you walk fast or climb stairs, your heart rate increases in appropriate increments. Imagine some ancient, intermediate species that kept passing out because its heart or lungs couldn't keep up. Or one who had to concentrate on where his tongue might be for every chew to avoid constant lacerations.

Nearly every living being has an incredible capability to monitor and repair itself. Many can regenerate lost or damaged parts such as most plants, lizards, octopi, and starfish; most species can repair their own DNA. Scientists have thus far identified 30 separate DNA repair mechanisms in humans. An accident? Blood can clot off wounds in cheetahs much the same as it does in humans. Burns to a rabbit's skin know how to repair themselves just as well as our own injuries; broken bones reconnect and regain their original strength in almost all species. Debris in the lungs is removed by specialized cells, irritants in the nose are sneezed away, problems in the throat or lungs are coughed up, troubles in the stomach are vomited, infections or toxins in the intestines are quickly expelled, and irritants on the skin are sloughed.

Most people know that our bodies will compensate with muscle building when one does increased work such as a graduated program of weight lifting. But plants do something similar. Add a reasonable weight to a limb so that it bends slightly. The tree will accommo-date and lift that weight back to level in time, or it will grow on the opposite side to accommodate that force.

If a person were to swallow a pebble by mistake, it would most likely pass through the intestines and easily exit unnoticed within a few days. Indeed, there are many oddball histories of mentally ill patients who have swallowed unusual items from toy trains to safety pins, nails, spoons, coins, doll heads, and razors. Drug smugglers called mules swallow bags of dope before crossing borders. Nearly all items pass through the entire gut without incident. Certainly, these items would never linger in one's stomach and change into useful and potentially critical parts of our physiology. There are many animals, however, who purposefully swallow rocks and retain them in their stomach to aid digestion. These foreign products are called gastroliths or gizzard stones, and they help animals grind up and pulverize seeds, husks, tough vegetable fiber, or shells in their stomachs. They are particularly helpful in many modern birds who lack teeth, but inexplicably, gastroliths can also be found in croco-diles and seals.

Typically, these are smooth, angular stones, free of the weathering or trauma which one might see if they were accidentally ingested. Also, they are quite different than the pebbles and rocks found in any nearby seabed. Scientists argue about their origins but most agree that they are a distinct functional phenomenon. They have been around for a long while.

The giant apatosaurus or brontosaurus dinosaurs ate leaves and other vegetation, presumably without chewing them, and then used these stones to break down the food much like our molars might. The stomach contents of plesiosaurs (prehistoric long-necked aquatic reptiles), suggest they ate in a similar, gulping manner. Their stom-achs include clam shell fragments, snail shells, and the hardened parts of belemnites, which may be an ancient relative to the cuttlefish or squid, to pulverize their food. Some scientists think that some of the seagoing monsters also used the stones for ballast.

There are hundreds, if not thousands, of improbable functions to write about. There are scores that can be found in anyone's backyard. One exotic example is the cape rain frog that lives in the sandy regions of Southern Africa. When seriously dry periods come, it gorges itself on water and then burrows deep into the sand to wait for the next rains.

There is the vampire catfish, the size of a skinny fifth finger, that attaches to fish gills and lives off the blood of much larger freshwater fish. The release of ammonia attracts them. Unfortunately, this same chemical will attract them to a person's urethra, should that person urinate in the water (consider yourself warned). They are very slippery and can slither partway inside. Their tiny pectoral fin acts like a barb preventing them from being pulled out. Surgery is the only solution.

Numerous fish, including the clown fish in *Finding Nemo,* sponges, brittle stars, and jellyfish can change sex as an adult. This primarily happens when there's a shortage of one sex or there's been a loss of a partner. Icelandic shrimp are all born as males and then 50 percent will change to females when they reach a certain size.

An invasive Mediterranean seaweed with fernlike fronds, sometimes called "killer algae," can reproduce itself from the tiniest fragments and heal any wound in seconds. The moment the plant has been injured, it releases an enzyme that activates caulerpenyne, a compound that it normally harbors. This compound recruits nearby algae proteins to the rupture site and another chemical called oxytoxin links them together in a tight bond.

Fishermen used to cut up nuisance starfish to kill them and then tossed the pieces overboard. Much to their chagrin, every piece made itself whole again and the numbers of starfish rapidly increased.

None of the foregoing are simple physiological phenomena that could have come about in one or two mutations.

15. ELECTRICITY AND BIOLUMINESCENCE

"LAB RULE #3:
In case of doubt,
make it sound convincing."

—ANONYMOUS

Every living thing is electrically charged. Trillions of electrical impulses travel along our nerve cells on a microsecond-by-microsecond basis, telling our brain what it needs to know about our environment and then relaying the appropriate responses to the entire body. Electrical impulses help regulate every organ system, impact every emotional state, and tell us when to sleep and when to wake. Every cell and every protein, perhaps every compound inside our body, makes use of electrical charges. Our health depends on it. Cells are like tiny batteries, and there are 10 to 75 trillion of them per person. In addition, each cell has dozens of generators called mitochondria. In some ways we are like skyscrapers with generators, batteries, and rechargers in every room.

A unique tissue in the heart called the SA node is the rate coordinator. Located in the right upper chamber, it sends electrical impulses to the interior muscles first and then the exterior muscles, telling them to contract, normally 60 to 100 times a minute. Exercise, low oxygen levels, and stress will cause the SA node to speed up; rest, which requires less oxygen, will cause the beating to slow down. A knee jerk is another classic electrical impulse. A thump on a certain spot below the kneecap will send an impulse to the spinal cord and back, bypassing conscious control and causing the knee to kick out. Its symmetric presence is considered to indicate good health. An absence could mean nerve damage. It may also mean the doctor didn't hit the right spot.

■ ■ ■ ■ ■

No one knows how electricity was originally incorporated into living beings, but some think life itself began with a lightning strike. There is some evidence that indirectly supports that notion. Whenever a person's heart stops, paramedics will shock the victim back to life. We declare someone dead when the electrical activity in their brain has ceased.

The question arises: Did the original lightning strike act like a pull cord on a lawn mower? Once the engine started, did it keep going, or did life require repeated lightning strikes, refueling, and maintenance? Incorporating electricity via the theory of evolution was not an easy step. Perhaps an impossible step?

UNDERWATER

About 500 aquatic species use electrical fields for mutual identification, scanning the environment, protection, hunting, killing, mating, and communications. Water is a better conductor than air, and electricity compensates for poorer visibility, but the range is usually limited to a few meters.

The most famous example has to be the electric eel. This denizen of the muddy Amazon and Orinoco rivers is not an eel at all, but more related to carp. It looks like an eel, however, and can grow to eight feet in length. Along its sides are three separate electric organs that can deliver a total shock of 350 to 650 volts in 1/500 of a second from its tail. This is enough voltage to stun a human being and kill any prey. Nerve cells stimulate electrical cells, called electroplaques, which are piled on top of each other like a stack of coins. Although each only has a 0.1 volt charge, together they can fire off an enormous charge. They have been known to fry equipment in their tanks.

There is no clear explanation in the theory of evolution.

The knife fish, which will often become an electric eel's dinner, also communicates by electrical impulses, and it has learned with time to vary the frequencies to keep eels from eavesdropping. Their electrical signals are primarily used to navigate and communicate. While mating, the male and female will sing an electrical duet.

The curlew-jawed mormyrid fish from South America uses an electric field to locate its prey. The leathery bill of a platypus creates an electrical field to locate shrimp and other food. The African electric fish emits a constant stream of electrical pulses between 300 and 400 per second. Its head is positively charged, and its tail is negative. The electric ray, once strapped to patients by ancient Romans to cure headaches, can blast a 200-volt charge from pectoral fins. It's about the only thing I haven't tried in my office for migraines. The stargazer fish buries all but its face in the sand and zaps passing prey from an electric organ between its eyes. Because of the difference in electrical conductivity, the physiologies of these species vary quite significantly between fresh and salt water.

Lights in the Water

The flashlight fish uses dense collections of green light-emitting bacteria in organs situated beneath each eye. The presumption is that they function like headlights to hunt for prey as well as communicate and escape predators. They have the ability to "close their eyelids" to turn the light off or send a signal. They are known to use a tactic of "blink and run" to avoid predators. They will blast their light, or lights as a group, and when the light stops and the visitor has re-adjusted, they have moved on. The Elsman whipnose swims upside down with a lantern-like illumination at the end of a long snout. The guess is that the light helps them find and attract worms. The hatchet fish emits a light-blue light along its underbelly as camouflage to simulate the weak sunlight from above to would-be predators.

Sharks, rays, and certain salamanders like axolotl do not have the ability to generate shocks, but they have a myriad of electroreceptor cells to detect changes around them. For example, sharks have tiny organs called ampullae of Lorenzini under their skin and in their snout that can detect electric fields as small as 0.005 millivolts. Rattlesnakes seem to pick up electrostatic charges with their tongue. A captured platypus will attack a live 1.5-volt battery in a pool and ignore a dead battery. There are major missing links throughout.

Bioluminescence is the ability to generate light, and it has "evolved" in 30 highly variable and unrelated species from mushrooms to fish, insects to jellyfish, and eyeless starfish to microorganisms. Some species make use of captured and groomed bacteria; others create their own light-emitting chemicals. Somehow, independent of each other, most use an enzyme called luciferase acting on luciferin and oxygen. Bioluminescence species can be found almost anywhere in the world, but it is particularly common in the oceans at depths below 500 feet where the sunlight cannot penetrate. These lights are used for communication, mutual identification, attracting prey, finding prey, confusing or scaring predators, and mating.

The most-often-cited example is the firefly, which is actually a beetle, not a fly, and can be found in the eastern parts of North America. Flying males flash a light from the tip of their tail to catch the attention of females on the ground. A response in kind begins their relationship. Certain predators, however, have learned to mimic these lights and will attract an excited male. Firefly lights come in yellows, blues, and greens and there are distinct signals for different species.

A midshipman fish communicates with bioluminescence generated by bacteria living in discs along its flanks that look like buttons on a midshipman's coat. It "sings" by vibrating muscles in its bladder that reportedly sound like the chant of Tibetan monks, and it can change frequencies for its own protection. When mating, as many as 30 male midshipman fish will sing in unison, sounding a bit like a motorboat, while the females watch from afar. Somehow, these females are able to select their mate from their singing.

The bobtail squid is another perplexing evolution. Within hours of hatching, it begins sucking in water through certain pores and selecting out a certain luminous vibrio bacteria. It eliminates all other bacteria and, in fact, eliminates any defective vibrio. Within 15 hours, millions of bacteria click on like a lightbulb. The amount of light and the size of the population is controlled by cells within these specialized organs. Somehow, despite the millions of bacteria types in the ocean, this squid can find, harvest, and groom the right bacteria.

■ ■ ■ ■ ■

The question arises as to whether electrical shocks and bioluminescence could have come about in small increments. This is much different than changing the bulb in a lamp. The chemistry and physiology that goes into accomplishing these feats and the number of brain cells needed to process it is enormous. It is also ineffective to have a barely visible light or an ineffective shock. This is an all-or-none phenomenon.

16. GROUNDSKEEPERS

"A true conservationist is a man who knows that the world is not given by his fathers, but borrowed from his children."

—JOHN JAMES AUDUBON

The mechanisms that take life apart came with the mechanisms that put life together. Or else our planet would have become uninhabitable long ago.

I have always been impressed by the cleanliness at popular parks like Disneyland and Butchart Gardens in Victoria, British Columbia. Despite a daily deluge of thousands of visitors, their walkways always look as if they were recently groomed. Armies of groundskeepers with brooms and other long-handled tools, trash containers, and a special eye for litter are responsible. Without them, visitors would be stepping over mounds of trash.

In a like manner, our world, which might be viewed as a giant amusement park, has an extensive array of natural groundskeepers. They are at work or on call 24/7/365, very eager to help out, typically quite prompt, and once on the job, incredibly thorough. They can take down anything from a whale carcass to the tiniest pine needle. These are not union members. Although there may be mandatory rest periods for some, there are no mandatory breaks or holidays off.

Some recyclers perish or are eaten so that the next shift can do their work—the price of business. Others linger for generations. They come in waves or shifts in a definite order with specific job descriptions, and they know how to utilize their tools, which include enzymes, heat, water, and oxygen. Flesh tends to belong to one group, bodily fluids to another, and hair or bones to still another. There are the first responders, the intermediate crews, and the final-touchers. They have their unique agenda, driven by survival, and without their combined and coordinated efforts, we would be climbing over mountains of dead animals from eons ago, sloshing through new excrement, and stepping on fossilized excrement of all kinds, swimming among billions of dead fish, crabs, and algae, drinking opaque slurries of various excrement and microorganisms, breathing air loaded with dried cells and flecks of animal waste, driving over stacked-up roadkill that had been smashed a thousand times over, and farming amidst monstrous mounds of dead crops.

Life would not be pleasant.

Imagine how your kitchen might look after a week's worth of unfinished meals and no clean-up. And that's nothing by comparison. After three billion years, the garbage dumpsites would dwarf Mt. Everest. Our survival depends upon the decomposition of all biodegradable trash, whether it be sloughed skin, lost feathers, or elephant dung. This partly is to make room to move about, but mostly to revitalize our air, soil, and seas. Our survival also depends on environmental processes to clean our air, seas, and soil. Oxygen (by coincidence?) is a great "burner" of waste.

■ ■ ■ ■ ■

Decay and decomposition cannot be done in half measures or be spread out over decades. These are exceedingly complex and interactive processes that are promptly accomplished by a long succession of scavengers; yet they are completed with seemingly relative ease. Just note how quickly a dead animal's body by the roadside will be picked clean.

Forensic medical examiners know that a homicide victim will have lost most of his or her flesh within six days. Using the normal sequence of arriving arthropods—there is a definable series of "my turn" with insects, the numbers of eggs laid and hatched, the degree of decomposition, and specific climate conditions—they can accurately determine the time of death. This can sometimes be done many days post mortem. We take these recycling processes for granted, but they are actually very complicated.

The first to arrive at a newly deceased animal may be the largest carnivores; indeed, they may even be the ones who dealt the fatal blow. Although humans might, by strict definition, be considered scavengers since we eat already-dead meat and dead plants, we try to keep our food as fresh as possible. We have our limits, whereas the larger, more typical scavengers like vultures, jackals, crows, and hyenas are not concerned about sell-by and expiration dates. Rotten meat is more like candy to vultures. They may come from miles away and even battle other creatures for the first bite of decaying flesh. Supposedly, sunken eyes are delicacies.

After the large scavengers remove the biggest chunks of flesh, a succession of rapidly proliferating insects and worms, plus billions of invisible bacteria, fungi, mold, and protozoa, take care of the rest. Should the deceased be a microorganism, there is a different succession of microscavengers, with the same end in sight.

In the sea, species such as sharks, barracudas, and piranhas are followed by a guest list that includes many types of arthropods (like crabs), worms, shrimp, and hordes of water-based bacteria, protozoa, algae, and fungi. Each group is like a team of groundskeepers at different parks. They wear different uniforms, eat slightly different meals, and have different ethnicity, but their jobs are the same. They are expected to return deceased life-forms to their basic units and feed themselves and their families as they go about it. Death and all biological trash is a buffet. They all work as a team with common goals.

Many other factors are at play as well. At the time of death, the immune systems that normally constrain and contain very dangerous bacteria in the intestines of all animals fail. These microbes immediately begin proliferating, invading nearby tissues, and dismantling their host from inside out. Preprogrammed? Bloating from the gases they produce is readily apparent in every corpse. At the same time, bacteria on the outside surfaces break through and start to work from the outside in. Skin, muscle, and organ tissues are quickly liquified. Bones take longer. Proteins, sugars, and fats are simplified and then internalized by the scavengers or converted to minerals, salts, carbon dioxide, oxygen, and water. Anything short of being thorough, the stench would be unbearable and disease rampant. Anything short of being thorough in past times would have halted the progression of life long before the age of dinosaurs.

The environment helps by drying out and oxidizing dead things on land. If it's warm outside, the process is sped up. The hotter it is, the faster it goes. Rain cleans the air and washes away biological breakdown products. Hydroxyl radicals clean the air. Winds blow dying leaves and twigs to the ground or knock down dying trees so the worms can begin a faster breakdown process. Waves in the seas break up sediment, thereby adding oxygen so it can be more easily broken down by other living organisms. Gravity pulls billions of tons of fish excrement and dead sea life to the floors of the oceans, where a huge group of scavengers are constantly at work.

Huge mucus balls also help feed deep-sea scavengers. Giant larvaceans, which resemble tadpoles, secrete huge mucus nets, up to a meter across, that capture food. Once they are too clogged with debris, they fall to the sea floor at a rate of 800 meters per day. Amphipods, tiny shrimplike creatures, survive on this kind of debris at the bottom of the Mariana Trench, 6.2 miles beneath the surface. In Monterey Bay, the bones from whale carcasses are decomposed by tube worms that will project green roots into the bones and then, using symbiotic bacteria, digest the oils. Multiple other bacteria attack the carcass. Most of a dead whale will be dismantled in days.

Even commercial outfits take advantage of the natural scavengers. Aquarium suppliers provide "attack packs" to clean aquariums, which include fancy serpent stars (tiger-striped or red), sand-sifting stars, sea cucumbers, burgundy sea stars, blue linckla sea stars, and brittle sea stars. They devour the biological trash, keeping their miniature world (amusement park?) clean.

INSECTS

Flies will start working on the deceased (or dung) within ten minutes of death—they can sense it somehow—and give birth to millions of maggots (miniature eating machines) within a day. They are followed by other types of flies, spiders, and beetles. Millions of maggots will cover a corpse within a few days. Some scavengers eat part of the carcass, and hide part for later. All expel the fecal products, which starts another cycle of smaller scavengers that may be eaten by carnivores and so on down and then back up the food chain. Among the missing links is how spiders eat. They secrete their digestive juices, and once their meal is liquefied, they suck the juice up like a kid with a straw in a soda-pop can. One wonders if predecessors had tried a host of digestive juices, starving all the while, until they genetically found the right one. It would have taken a massive mutation to create these processes and have them all work together so nicely.

According to Dr. Gilbert Waldbauer, most of the members in 18 of the 32 orders of insects are scavengers. They include cockroaches, ants, certain caterpillars, blowflies, flesh flies, select butterflies that suck fluids from bodies, moths that eat hair, and many different types of beetles. Fire ants collect flesh from vertebrate carcasses and dine on other dead insects. Maggots secrete an antibiotic that will kill competing bacteria. Silverfish, not really an insect group of their own, like dying wood products; eating my old books is one of their jobs.

Burying beetles will bury mammals as large as a mouse with hopes of using them for long-term food supply. There are 75 species of these burying beetles and they are in strict competition with millions of other insects. They also move quickly in hopes of avoiding their competition: bears, coyotes, skunks, snails, turkey vultures, and coyotes. They will use these hidden carcasses for months to feed their kin. No concern about discard dates. Biologists report that they, like birds, regurgitate partially digested portions of the flesh and feed it to their larvae, who stand up on their hind legs to be fed. For most of us, that's an endearing image.

RECYCLING

Although the excrement of all living beings must be recycled, relatively little is known about the process. About 40 percent of what we eat goes out the other end. It is rich in the nutrients that both insects and bacteria need, maybe enjoy. According to Waldbauer, 19 species of dung beetles are attracted to the excrement of wooly monkeys in Colombia's Tinigua National Park. The owlet moth caterpillar of Florida lives in gopher tortoise burrows and lives off their dung. The fly genus Scatophaga (dung-eater) will fight over territory on cow patties, while as many as 150 different successive fly and beetle species may make a 9-inch patty their temporary home. Certain beetles will dig a hole beneath the dung to bury it, others will make a large ball bigger than themselves and roll it to their nest or another burrow, and some, called kleptoparasites, will steal dung from other beetles. Once the patty has been buried, they move it to a newer pile.

All vegetation needs to be recycled. Earthworms, roundworms, millipedes, and insects play major roles by grinding up fallen leaves and dead plants in their digestive systems and then passing millions of fecal pellets, which are further decomposed by a myriad of bacteria, protozoa, and fungi. While these decomposers thrive, other scavengers like centipedes, spiders, and salamanders thrive on them. Pools of water with detritus (rotting stuff or plant litter) are likely to be loaded with tiny fly larvae called midges, bacteria, protozoa, earthworms, several types of microscopic shrimp, and water fleas. Over time they will turn this nutritional muck into the basic units— minerals, proteins, amino acids, water, and carbon dioxide.

Every living being must die and every living being must be recycled. It's a given. This is truly an all-or-none phenomenon—perhaps a

Mandatory Plan. There are a number of missing-link questions. How does a living being recognize dead tissue? Is it by smell, sound, sight, chemical signal, communication from other species, or all of the above? When and how does a scavenger ingest the different decaying remnants? What chemical processes need to be in place to keep the digesters from becoming digested themselves or getting ill? Where does it end—meaning scavengers have smaller scavengers and they, in turn, have smaller scavengers? Could this multitiered spiral balancing act have happened on its own?

The "dust to dust" phenomenon is very well orchestrated and incredibly complex. These are not accidental or random events. Hundreds of different species among scores of different species of all sizes and shapes participate, using uncountable processes to feed and metabolize life's products. This is their job; this is their life. Darwin's theory of evolution does not address the decay and decomposition cycle in any depth. It is, indeed, clearly filled with many missing links. Every aspect of life could not have a beginning without an ending. It goes full circle. Science presently draws this circle with a dotted line.

One cannot assume a recycling plant appeared on the outskirts of a town by accident. Nor can one assume that it evolved and was functional as a half-built structure. And likewise, every aspect of Nature's recycling smacks of Intelligent Planning.

17. SYMBIOSIS

"We are symbionts on a symbiotic
planet, and if we care to, we can find
symbiosis everywhere. Physical
contact is a non-negotiable requisite
for many differing kinds of life."

—LYNN MARGULIS, PHD,
AUTHOR OF **SYMBIOTIC PLANET**

S*ymbiosis* describes an unusually close or mandatory association between two or more unrelated species for their mutual survival. The word was taken from the Latin *sym,* meaning together, and *bios,* meaning life. Many textbooks often cite lichens as a prime example. These plantlike entities are composed of algae, which make food from sunlight, and fungi, which provide water and protection. Neither species can survive on their own. How they became so entwined, however, is unknown. How they even existed (if they did) as single entities beforehand is only a guess.

Symbiosis should not be confused with *commensalism,* which means eating at the same table. For example, there's a worm that rooms with a hermit crab. It even shares the same meals, but as best as scientists can tell, they are merely an odd couple. Another extremely bizarre, dot-sized animal called *Symbion pandora* lives inside a Norwegian lobster's mouth, where it vacuums up passing food particles for itself and reproduces by growing a youngster out its own rear end. It can also produce a dwarf male that is only a brain and reproductive organs. No one has the faintest idea what group of animals this species belongs to or how it came about.

■ ■ ■ ■ ■

Symbiosis is the opposite of *parasitism,* wherein one species will be detrimental to the other's health. This kind of taking advantage can be readily seen in a tapeworm infection, malaria, typhoid, and even athlete's foot. An extremely unusual and unexplained example is the cordyceps fungus, which lies waiting on the forest floor, attaches itself to a passing insect, burns a hole through the exoskeleton, and eats all of the nonvital tissues plus a particular part of the brain. This causes the insect to climb to the top of the highest tree available. The fungus then eats the rest of the brain and causes the insect to split open, whereupon the fungus releases its spores into the wind. An accident?

Another model of parasitism is the freshwater mussel. Found throughout the United States, these bivalves will extrude and wave about a minnow-like part of their body. When the right species of fish comes to take the bait, it explodes thousands of larvae into the predator's mouth. They attach to the fish's gills and live there, sucking its blood, sometimes for months, and then fall off when mature enough to become bivalves in the riverbed.

MUTUAL DEPENDENCE

Just the fact that we require oxygen from plants and they require carbon dioxide from us tells us most of life is a symbiotic relationship. Our families have a type of symbiotic relationship, as do our co-workers and teammates. Depending on another species is quite common in Nature.

The oxpecker bird, with its specially shaped beak and stiff tail for propping itself when at work, removes ticks and fleas from camels, giraffes, rhinos, and buffalos. These birds are particularly drawn to the eyes, ears, and anus—everyone, except pesky insects, benefits. The Douglas fir beetle uses a fungus to plug up its burrow holes; the fungus uses the beetles' leftovers for food. Certain shrimp clean the dwellings of gobi fish, which in turn warn the shrimp about approaching predators. The acremonium fungus protects fescue grass by giving it a bitter taste. Gutless mussels offer protection to

■■ LIFE CYCLE OF MUSSELS ■■

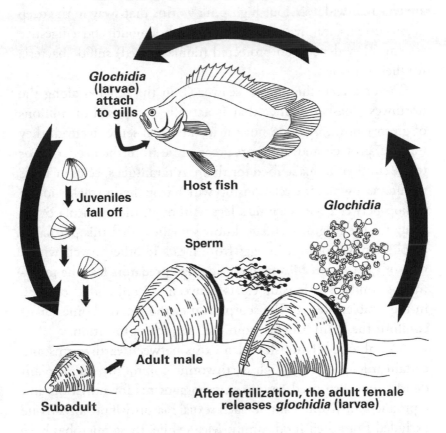

Variations on a theme. Mussels have several ways of sending out their larvae to a host fish's gills. One of them is dangling fancy wormlike lures and then squirting larvae in a fish's face when it approaches. Mussels' complex life cycle requires two hosts and could not have evolved in separate stages.

Illustration by Dana Csakany

certain bacteria in exchange for food that they make. Rifia, which are ten-inch-wide, six-foot-high pink worms that sway in the deep ocean currents near hydrothermal vents, lack a mouth and a digestive system. They depend on protected (domesticated) sulfide bacteria for their nutrition.

There's a recurring green "seaweed" on the beaches along the northwest coast of France that is actually composed of millions of green worms. They do not eat in the usual sense; instead, they nurture, protect, and transport green algae from the deeper sands to the sunlight to make food for them. A tarantula species in Texas maintains a symbiotic relationship with a frog that is small enough to hop between the arachnid's legs. Although the tarantula could easily eat the frog, it seems to know somehow that this particular amphibian will protect its eggs from flies and other insects with a flick of the tongue. Meanwhile, the frog's predators fear the tarantula. A similar relationship exists between a lizard and a scorpion in the Arabian desert. The scorpion uses the lizard's home for its comfort; the lizard benefits from the scorpion's protection.

A symbiotic relationship also exists between earthworms and certain microbes. Although earthworms commonly ingest plant debris, they also need certain microorganisms for nutrition and reproduction. Worms cannot reach sexual maturity if protozoans are excluded from their food supply. Meanwhile, these microbes have the pleasure of being expelled in nutrient-rich casts. Were these two species loners who found each other eons ago?

Just to complicate this, studies have shown that the antibiotic doxycycline cures a certain parasitic disease called elephantiasis, caused by a mosquito bite. Unchecked, this tiny worm causes lymph node scarring, which leads to massive and grotesque swellings of legs or genitals (wheelbarrow size). So, what's the big deal? Antibiotics often kill pathogens. The antibiotic, however, doesn't affect the parasite at all. Instead, it kills a bacteria called wucheria that lives inside the worm. When the microbe dies, so does the parasite. They have a mandatory, symbiotic relationship.

There are mice that travel around with beetles clamped to their fur like necklaces or brooches. These beetles eat fleas that infect mice habitats—a meal in exchange for protection. Wolbachia bacteria, a common symbiont in insects, can actually change the sex of the host insect's offspring.

The vanilla flavoring found in your kitchen cupboard is a consequence of symbiosis. The vanilla bean comes from an orchid plant that can only be pollinated by a tiny stinger-free, flea-sized bee that knows how to go under a minute septum and take the pollen to the next plant. For 300 years Europeans repeatedly failed to grow this plant; now they do it by artificial insemination. Making things even more difficult is the fact that there's only a three-hour window when this flower stays open. This special bee and very unique plant had to have originated together.

RESIDENT BACTERIA

Humans depend on certain bacteria in our small intestines for the manufacture of vitamin K. Without their work, our blood would never clot and the smallest of injuries might cause us to bleed to death. Pregnancy and childbirth would be a fatal affliction, and perhaps the human race would not have survived. These same microorganisms, in turn, depend upon our food intake for their own nutrition.

A different set of intestinal bacteria keep the more dangerous, toxin-producing microorganisms at bay. It appears as if H. pylori bacteria, often blamed for causing stomach ulcers, may be protective against salmonella and other worrisome bacteria. Women depend on a specific bacteria lactobacillus within their vagina to protect them from candida (yeast) infections. Certain benign staphylococcal colonies in our tears may keep the much more dangerous chlamydia bacteria away. Other bacterial strains who reside in our nasal passages keep streptococcus out. There is even some evidence that a certain bacteria may influence the normal development of blood vessels in the bowels.

There are studies suggesting that we require certain kinds of bacterial exposure as children to best develop our immune systems. The suggestion is that we wash our hands a little too much or use disinfectants too often. Diseases such as asthma and inflammatory bowel disease are clearly on the rise, and some professionals believe it's partly because we keep our homes and our kids way too sterile. Supposedly, these early childhood exposures prime our immune system and help us fight diseases as an adult. Although no one is telling us to let the dishes pile up or keep flies in our homes, there may be reasons to revisit our obsession with cleanliness.

We are all born with a sterile gut, meaning no bacteria can be found in the intestines. That's why a baby's waste doesn't smell and pregnant women don't succumb to infections from their baby. Imagine a baby without that design, carrying bacteria that could injure mom. With bacteria on board, a baby would quickly become a deep, life-threatening abscess. These microorganisms begin to populate our small intestine after the first month and eventually number in the zillions; they come from a variety of sources, but mostly from mother's body. Somehow, they know where to go and not go, or our bodies know how to direct or control them. The safer and more useful ones get in and the dangerous ones are kept away or under lock and key.

Medical journals have been warning medical doctors and hospitals about a newer, more deadly version of a gut bacteria called *Clostridia difficile*. Normally, it is kept in check by our bacteria communities in our small intestines, but when antibiotics are given for a specific illness like pneumonia, the good gut bacteria are also killed off. This line of defense has been broached. *C. difficile* quickly multiplies, possibly as much as 17 million progeny (offspring) in 24 hours. Severe, disabling diarrhea follows with high fevers; the colon blows up like a balloon and can perforate. This disease is bad enough, but the newest version is resistant to our usual therapies. In 2005, it killed a 31-year-old, six-month pregnant woman with twins who had merely been treated for a bladder infection.

We need these "good guys" for survival and they need us.

SINE QUA NON RELATIONSHIPS

According to evolutionary theory, insects evolved from carnivores (scavengers) who couldn't digest plants. How would that logically happen? There is strong evidence that some, and maybe most, insects make use of microbes residing in their stomachs to digest those leaves they seem to love so much. Helpful and necessary yeast can be found in the guts of sap-sucking insects. Many insects also have microorganisms in their intestines to detoxify plant chemicals.

Unbelievably, termites, who eat wood from downed trees for sustenance, cannot actually digest wood. They require a protozoan found in their hindgut to break the cellulose down. Without this symbiotic relationship they would starve to death. Newborn termites pick up these protozoa, called mixotrichs, by eating their parents' anal droppings. One wonders how Darwinists can explain how they learned to do this. Termites will also lose their personal protozoa when molting and then recapture new ones from the rear ends of friends and relatives.

This story thickens, however. There is evidence to suggest that the

Spotters

There is a century-old story about a raven and a mountain lion that highlights a different kind of symbiosis. Supposedly a woman was hanging out her wash when a raven began frantically squawking and flapping about her head. Looking around, she realized a mountain lion was eyeing her, presumably for dinner, from a distance. She quickly ran to her house and got her husband, who shot the animal. Newspapers across the country raved how this glorious raven had saved her life. A few decades later, however, an expert on ravens dispelled that notion. It turns out ravens work with mountain lions as spotters and then, as a reward for a good job, they get to partake in the pickings after the kill. A symbiotic relationship.

The honeyguide, or black-throated indicator bird, of the African rain forests performs a similar task. It loves the taste of honey and bee larvae, but being the size of a common lark, it shows the honey badger (who can break open the nest) where to find them. The bird has also been seen tracking down Pygmies and leading them to a nest. Pygmies always make sure there are leftovers for their guides.

mixotrich protozoa cannot get around inside the termite intestines (to eat the wood) without numerous, whiplike tails that actually belong to tiny bacteria attached to their outer wall.

One wonders what the chances are that this three-tiered symbiotic relationship could have happened by accident.

Another multitiered symbiotic relationship exists between certain ants, aphids, and millions of buchnera bacteria. Ants manage aphids like a dairy farmer might care for his cows. In exchange for protection, these domesticated aphids make a nutritious, sugary foodstuff for the ant colony. The buchnera, who live within the aphid intestines, help the aphids manufacture their life-sustaining proteins.

A paramecium is a unicellular microorganism commonly found in every pond. It collects and transports algae to lighted areas to make food for both of them. The Hawaiian squid relies on a light-emitting bacteria to find food. Jellyfish found in the lakes on the Palau Islands harbor green algae, which they carry to the sunlight in order to make food for the both of them.

UNDERGROUND ASSISTANCE

Many plants depend on nitrogen-fixing bacteria, while many nitrogen-fixing bacteria depend on the same plants for products of photosynthesis. Bury a seed anywhere and the right bacteria or right fungus will somehow find it and link up in the correct way. A mismatch can easily lead to stunted growth or even the seed's demise.

Nearly all trees and most of our crops depend on extensive underground biological systems created by mycorrhizal fungi. These crisscrossing stringlike filaments can penetrate soil much deeper and more thoroughly than most roots. They capture and then exchange phosphate and other minerals for the root's sugary sap. The same kind of fungi help with drought tolerance and pest resistance. One root fungus called *Trichoderma harzianum* coils around disease-causing microbes and sucks their vital fluids dry.

Underground fungal systems can be found nearly everywhere from the Arctic to the tropics. They cannot exist—or at least science has not found a single species that grows—independently. They need the plants as much as the plants need them.

In his book *Liaisons of Life*, Tom Wakeford describes a very revealing experiment:

> Over forty years ago, Swedish botanist Erik Björkman provided the first evidence for connective capacities of mycorrhizae when he injected radioactive glucose into the trunk of a Norway spruce tree and then measured it being transferred to a neighboring plant. Despite his suggestion that mycorrhizal fungi were responsible for this dramatic effect, few understood its potential significance. Björkman's findings seemed to fly in the face of all conventional evolutionary theory, in which individuals compete to get the maximum benefit for themselves from a common pool of resources, thereby depriving others—the principle of "the survival of the fittest."

One might think it's merely adult or older trees helping their own species, but studies in the 1990s by Suzanne Simard of Oregon State University indicate trees help different species. Birch and fir trees will share as many as ten fungal symbionts and send sugar to smaller trees. And these fungi always benefit from sap sugars. They may tap as much as 30 percent of the tree's production.

There are many other underground symbiont microorganisms. Rhizobia, for example, is a very common bacteria that is responsible for forming nitrogen-providing nodules on the roots of bean plants. They convert soil nitrogen into the building blocks of proteins. This is a very difficult chemical step for most plants and a very vital step in our own existence. In exchange, the plant provides them sugar and amino acids for nutrition and an oxygen blanket for protection from anaerobic predators.

■ ■ ■ ■ ■

There are many variations on these traditional symbiotic themes and even the simplest defy an evolutionary explanation. One question that readily arises is, how could certain species have ever survived alone or even come about if they needed major help? Or why did they link up with another species in such a way that they could never extricate themselves again without dying? And how did they even find such an extremely compatible partner? For evolution theory to explain these dilemmas, there had to have been uncountable physiological problems, anatomical incompatibilities, and scores of trials and errors until the right pair linked up in the right way. One might liken this to a diabetic trying to find his lost medications in the Sahara Desert.

Science is relatively silent on these issues.

18. MIGRATION

"[Birds are] actually aware of the flight conditions that they're under; they're able to, as we realize from our [satellite radar] results, abandon a certain direction of flight if things are getting too rough for them, and they make landfall somewhere, where, perhaps, they wouldn't have done if things had been different. So, they're negotiating the journey."

—DR. PETER DRISCOLL,
QUEENSLAND WADER STUDY GROUP

Imagine spending several weeks loading up on fatty foods and then walking nonstop from Seattle to Los Angeles to spend the winter. Once there, you quickly fall in love, immediately have children, fatten up again, and then return to Seattle for the summer. Meanwhile, your fast-track kids grow up in L.A. (without you), fatten up at fast-food mills and, before summer gets too hot, they also walk to Seattle without the apparent help of a map, road signs, a relative, or even a guide. Sounds ridiculous—and for humans, of course it is, but this is somewhat representative of what millions of animals do every year. Rather than hibernate or tough it out during the cold seasons, they travel to milder climates. They prepare for this journey with incredible thoroughness and they complete it with impeccable precision. Many do it without ever having been to the other home before.

■■■■■

In the seventeenth century the Bishop of Herford published *The Man in the Moone: Discourse of a Voyage Thither*, in which he said people could harness a ship to birds and fly to the moon. During the nineteenth century many people believed that swallows burrowed into holes for the winter. Communication, or lack of it, was such that there was no way to know if a bird had flown thousands of miles or a fish had swum hundreds. Certain species just seemed to magically disappear and reappear around the same time every year.

Most of us do not have much more of a sophisticated view of migration: Birds fly south in the winter to escape the ravages of cold weather and north in the summer to reap the benefits of warmer weather (in the northern hemisphere). We've all heard of Canada geese migrating across our country and the extremely punctual swallows of San Juan Capistrano, but there are many different species besides birds that migrate. Among them are caribou, eels, lobsters, fish, butterflies, walruses, ladybugs, moths, ants, termites, dragonflies, penguins, turtles, tortoises, locusts, zebras, wildebeests, bats, whales, and certain bacteria.

ALMOST UNBELIEVABLE

Some of the distances traveled are unbelievable. Baby loggerhead turtles migrate 8000 miles across the Atlantic Ocean. The arctic tern flies 25,000 miles per year, the longitudinal length of the Earth and back again. The blackpoll warbler has been seen as high as 21,000 feet, traveling over two major bodies of water. Other impressive journeys include the graying goose (1800 miles), the Eurasian crane (2500 miles), the white stork (3100 miles), the bobolink (6000 miles), the whooper swan (1500 miles), the bald eagle (1800 miles), the snow goose (2500 miles), the rockhopper penguin (620 miles), and the Brazilian free-tailed bats from Carlsbad Caverns into Mexico (800 miles). A banded albatross once flew around the world in less than 80 days.

The migration of the monarch butterfly is among the more miraculous journeys and one that is truly hard to explain. More than a hundred million butterflies fly from northern North America to a small grove of oyamel firs on a remote central Mexican mountain 2500 miles away, yet not a single one of them has ever made this trip before. Going several generations back, the first monarch to arrive in North America lived long enough to mate and lay eggs (about a month). Subsequent generations also mated and died, yet somehow the precise coordinates for the oyamels were passed on, over and over again. For some reason the last generation knew they were the chosen ones to make the trip. They knew how much nectar to convert to fats, not to mate this time, and how to get to a very specific place in central Mexico.

No one truly knows how this came about.

Biology texts are loaded with other unbelievable accounts. During a three-quarter moon in December, over 200,000 female olive ridley turtles come ashore to lay their eggs along a remote half-mile stretch of a beach in Costa Rica. The event is called *la arribada*, the arrival. They travel hundreds of miles from North America, South America, and the open sea.

A Topic of Ignorance

Many animals endure incredible hardships just to survive another year, reproduce, and find alternative sources of food. Yet these incredibly complex journeys are almost entirely ignored in the evolution literature. The old theory that the scarcity of food caused some species to migrate and as those food sources diminished, the species began making bigger and bigger loops loses some credibility when one studies birds that fly thousands of miles over open water. Certain hummingbirds migrate 500 to 650 miles across open seas from North America to Central America.

The spiny lobster larva at 0.06 inches hitchhikes on a tiny jellyfish. It will travel up to thousands of miles and may molt as many as 11 times. Both the hitchhiking and the molting were never viewed beforehand, yet they all know how.

The North American and European eels are hatched in the Sargasso Sea near the West Indies. They travel the length of North America or across the Atlantic Ocean. It takes them about 7 to 10 years to mature into silver eels, at which time they all return to their birthplaces to mate again. Somehow they remember, learn, or follow internal directions.

Every summer hundreds of millions of ladybug beetles migrate from the hot deserts of Arizona to the cooler Santa Clara Mountains in California where they estivate. Before they leave they fatten up on aphids to make the journey and sustain them through that season.

PREPARATION, TIMING, AND GUIDANCE

Every species seems to know how to prepare for the arduous trip far in advance, but no one knows how they acquire this capability. If it's inherited, which is the logical assumption, does knowing what to eat, how much to eat, how much to drink, how to find food and water, how much to weigh, how much preening oil is needed, and how to compensate for opposing winds, downdrafts, and rainstorms all show up at the same time by a massive set of simultaneous mutations? Along with the ability to go without sleep, a keen sense of direction, night vision, and powerful wings or fins? Or could these different aspects have shown up separately as useless, successive functions? One would think all these preparations had to have come as a whole package. There is way too much purposeful change for random mutations. Many aspects are not at all compatible with survival of the fittest.

Some birds have an uncanny ability to depart and arrive at very precise times or locations. San Juan Capistrano swallows always touch down at the old Mission in California on March 19, St. Joseph's Day. Tourists can literally adjust their calendars by it. Barn swallows are famous for returning to exactly the same rafter in the same barn, year after year.

Not only do certain species travel thousands of miles repeating the precise routes that their parents and grandparents had traveled before them, they also seem to know the locations of watering holes along the way. That final destination might be a tiny island in a vast sea, the tip of a peninsula thousands of miles away, a set of trees on a narrow landscape, a series of sea cliffs, or the base of a mountain on a distant continent. Yet nearly all find their new/old home every time. The migration might take days, weeks and, in some species, years. Could they have been born with fully functional GPS systems intact from the beginning?

The pigeon-size plover is a phenomenal example. They breed in Siberia and Alaska and then travel up to 13,000 miles to islands in the Pacific and Indian Oceans. They do this in roughly 90 continuous hours, burn off one third to one half their body weight, go without sleep or food, and arrive at the same island their parents left. Since they cannot swim, there is no possibility of stopping en route.

We know that some birds use the sun, moon, and stars to guide them. Many species such as baby loggerhead turtles, salmon, honey-bees, whales, homing pigeons, frogs, Zambian mole rats, and some bacteria use magnetic clues. An experiment by William T. Keeton of Cornell University once proved that blindfolded pigeons could easily find their way home. When tiny magnets were hung around their neck and the blindfolds removed, however, they could not.

Magnetotactic bacteria use the earth's geomagnetic fields for migration, albeit a much shorter journey. These organisms were discovered in 1975 by Richard Blakemore, when he observed that certain bacteria always moved across the slide toward a magnet. They line up iron-containing, magnetic particles inside their bodies and use them like a compass. In the northern hemisphere, the bacteria travel toward the true North Pole, and in the southern hemisphere toward the true South Pole. Since these angles are also downward, the prevailing thought is that they need an oxygen-poor environment found in deeper waters.

■ ■ ■ ■ ■

Migration is an arduous journey. Birds often burn more calories than they can store and go without sleep. Imagine running for three or four days straight without stopping. They make use of wind currents, dodge foul weather, fly in formation, and conserve energy. If the different migration processes came about slowly by trial and error, as Darwinian theory would have one believe, birds would be dropping out of the sky from exhaustion everywhere. And then, of course, there would be the ripple effect on the ecology of every region they frequented. Birds help keep the insect populations in check, fertilize the plants, sow the seeds, and decorate the statues.

One might say, with good reason, that we could not exist without them.

19. HIBERNATION, ESTIVATION, AND SLEEP

"I have never let my schooling
interfere with my education."

—MARK TWAIN

When food becomes scarce during the colder seasons and energy must be conserved, many mammals, certain birds, and some insects will go into dormancy or hibernation. These prolonged bouts of inactivity are genetically hard-wired modes of survival. Most people think both types of sleep are the same, but true hibernators will drastically lower their temperatures, do not wake to forage, and remain hard to arouse until the correct moment. If the latter were to be awakened prematurely, there could be disastrous consequence. The sudden expenditure of energy to rouse taps into limited (preprogrammed) fat stores, and they may not have enough reserve to warm up at the proper time.

The physiological changes required for prolonged sleep are extremely complex. Nearly every cell, organ system, and metabolic pathway in an animal is involved. A groundhog will slow its heart rate from 80 beats per minute (bpm) to a barely life-supporting 4 bpm and its temperature from 38° C (100° F) to 7° C (45° F); the ground squirrel will lower its pulse from 150 bpm to 5 bpm and its temperature from 32.1° C (90° F) to 4.4° C (40° F). They look dead.

Skunks, bears, and raccoons will wake intermittently to find food (therefore, they are not "true hibernators") and then go right back to sleep. Hummingbirds hibernate only at night when temperatures drop. This is called nocturnal hibernation or torpor; this is a required temporary state. They use too many calories eating on the wing during the day to store any for the night, plus they are unable to see flowers at night. Allen's hummingbird will use 30 times less oxygen at night than during the day. Amazingly, a bat can drop its heart rate of 1000 bpm in flight to 25 bpm during hibernation, its rate of breathing to one breath every two hours, and its temperature by 20° C (36° F). Bears will drop their temperature by four degrees; smaller animals might drop 30° C.

■ ■ ■ ■ ■

The preparation that goes into hibernating is enormous. It cannot have evolved one step at a time in different species. From the moment these animals wake from a long sleep, they restart building fat stores for the next sleep. Instinctively, they know what to eat, how to find it, how much to store, when there's enough socked away, and when it's time to pull the sheets up again. Their anatomy and physiology are geared for these kinds of complex life changes.

Whether it be a burrow, a cave, a crevice in a wall, or a stump, hibernators also know to find and properly prepare their sleeping chamber. Being relatively vulnerable, they need to be protected from the adverse climate and predators. As their sleep begins, every cell in their body will slow down in a controlled, synchronized manner. Some animals maintain a warmer inner core while their exterior is quite cold to the touch. According to Corine Lacrampe, author of *Sleep and Rest in Animals,* "Despite the work of scientists in examining the sleep of about 150 species of mammals, we still do not fully understand sleep's real function or that of REM sleep and dreams."

Bears drop their oxygen consumption by 50 percent. Calories are burned more slowly, heart rates and blood pressures drop, and kidney function diminishes. Even the intestines prepare by lining the walls with large numbers of white cells that stand guard and protect the hibernator from the bacteria within. Imagine every resident of

Tokyo or New York City simultaneously turning their thermostat down one degree at a time and then simultaneously turning their lights off.

▄▄ WHITE CELL ATTACKING BACTERIA ▄▄

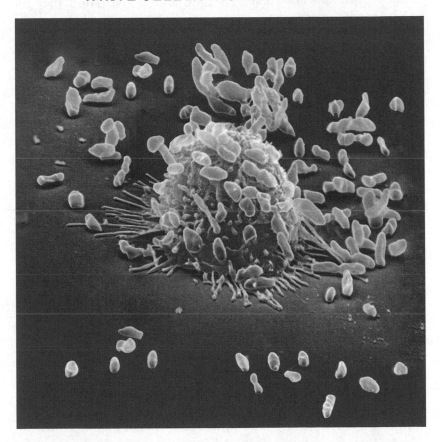

Human white cells attack bacteria continually throughout the body. They make use of very sophisticated chemical and physical weapons. How they learned what to attack, and how they learned to attack bacteria, are wholly unexplained by the theory of evolution.

© David M. Phillips / Photo Researchers, Inc.[6]

Medical Hibernation

Doctors have discovered that copying the physiology of hibernation may be useful when treating the critically ill. Victims of head injuries are sometimes kept at lower temperatures to allow the brain to heal and slow the damage. The Fred Hutchinson Cancer Center has used the gas hydrogen sulfide in experiments on mice. They were able to lower their temperatures from 98° F to 59° F and their breathing rate from 120 per minute to less than 10 per minute. Afterwards, the mice were revived and appeared healthy. Something like this will very likely be a future treatment modality.

Many questions arise: Can hibernation be an accident of evolution or accomplished by trial and error? For example, could the bears' ancestors have tried sleeping different lengths of time (and survived) until they got it right and then passed the proper directions onto their offspring? This would require incalculable genetic modifications. What keeps bears as strong as they were when they went to sleep months earlier? If one were to put a man to bed for a couple of weeks, he would soon be "as weak as a kitten." Bears may lose 20 percent of their strength, but they can still tear an intruder apart within seconds of rousing. Studies show that hibernating bears actually go through intermittent, violent muscle contractions resembling chills which may be preprogrammed isometric exercises. They also have near-absolute control over urine and bowels, and a mother can nurse five to seven months without drinking because her fat is automatically changed to water and nutrients. Another accident of Nature?

Hibernation was once thought to be a physiological failure or throwback to reptiles. In other words, some warm-blooded hibernators had not yet escaped a primitive need to shut down when the temperature dropped. Indeed, on the surface the physiology of some cold-blooded animals may seem similar, but reptilian physiology is much simpler than that of warm-blooded species. These animals' core temperatures, even at extreme times, are usually higher than the environment and well-controlled, whereas a reptile simply becomes a frozen reptile.

A SUMMER'S SLEEP

Summer hibernation is called *estivation*, and it provides a way for select species to survive the excessively hot months. In a manner not unlike winter hibernators, their metabolism is slowed and shelter sought, but the physiological changes are not quite as drastic.

The West African and Congolese lungfish are classic examples. They live in marshes that dry out with the heat. They survive by secreting a thick, hardening mucus casing that keeps them moist and alive for months. They can also take in low levels of oxygen without lungs; their nourishment becomes a self-cannibalism, called autophagy, wherein they break down their own muscle tissues; and their kidneys can store waste products at 2000 times the average vertebrate. Natives seeking a lungfish meal will mimic the sounds of a rainstorm by tapping on the ground, listen for the telltale grunts in response, and dig the fish up.

One wonders how the lungfish could have partially developed the right amount and type of casing by trial and error. It would never survive to reproduce on something less adapted. Is the fact that its kidneys shut down without going into permanent failure a fluke of nature? If a human kidney shuts down, it can lead to fatal consequences.

Other animals that estivate include land crabs, earthworms, and snails. The desert snail can estivate for five years. One of the best-known mammals to estivate is the tenrec, a hedgehog-type of animal from Madagascar. It can estivate in the summer or hibernate in the winter, depending on the temperature changes. Zoos once noticed how stiff and cold they became when housed in cooler environments.

REGULAR SLEEP

Do we sleep because we are tired? Of course, most everyone would respond, but there are reasons to think that sleeping has more to do with the brain's need to reorganize than actually resting the body. For example, orca whales and some dolphins will stay awake for a month after giving birth. They keep nudging their newborn to the surface to take a breath every 30 seconds. One would think, if sleep was designed to reverse fatigue only, these mothers would eventually sink from exhaustion.

Elephants sleep four hours per night, yet they carry enormous weight around in the heat. One would think this would be enormously tiring and they might need more sleep than most animals. The okapi, which is a small giraffe-like animal, needs only 20- to 30-second naps for a total of 5 minutes sleep in 24 hours. A giraffe sleeps a total of two hours, getting about 20 minutes of REM sleep in 1- to 6-minute periods while lying down. The Indus dolphin never sleeps. Other dolphins sleep with half a brain and one eye closed, while the other half-brain and eye keep watch. Hippos sleep underwater, yet they automatically surface to breathe air about every six minutes without waking.

A person can spend the entire night lying in bed awake, essentially resting every muscle, bone, and organ, yet rise in the morning feeling exhausted. For unclear reasons, the brain desperately needs a period of changed brain waves. Rats deprived of sleep for three weeks will die. To encourage us to get some sleep, the brain sends us signals we are physically tired. This is followed by an overwhelming need to sleep; we yawn, doze off, and eventually collapse if we don't listen to the clues.

The question comes up, however—is our body truly exhausted? The winner of a marathon race doesn't doze on the medal stand or tell the press they need to take a nap before the interview. Weight lifters and Olympic swimmers don't take naps at the end of competition. Yet newborn babies, who are not competing, sleep constantly. Are they exhausted, or is this a function of development? More likely it's the latter. Sleep appears to be something more than rest—something uniquely needed by the brain.

Sleep, in some species, is dictated by the third eye, or pineal gland, which responds to the amount of light present and secretes a hormone called melatonin. In fish, amphibians, and reptiles it is often located at the top of the head where it can "see" the sunlight. In birds it is found inside the brain. We have a comparable tissue deep within the brain that reacts to light forwarded mostly by our eyes.

It appears as if all birds go through REM (Rapid Eye Movement) sleep. The owl's eyes, however, remain fixed even though the brain shows the characteristic changes of REM sleep. Reptiles, amphibians, and fish do not seem to have REM sleep. No one can explain where REM started in evolution and why.

Charles Amlaner from Indiana State University has shown that mallards, when feeling threatened, will sleep with half their brain and one eye open. When sleeping in flocks, birds on the fringe sleep with one eye open. Many birds either sleep on the wing or don't sleep while taking long journeys, such as swifts, eagles, and albatrosses. Accident or Design?

Cold-weather sleepers like frogs will settle in mud at the bottom of a pool to stay warm; garter snakes will huddle by the thousands. The brains of seals sleeping underwater only show slow waves; they get their REM sleep for a few minutes at the surface. Dolphins do not have REM sleep. Again, no one knows why.

Automatic Adjustments

All of our bodily functions are maintained and adjusted during the time we sleep. Metabolism slows, temperature falls to subnormal, heart rates drop, and blood pressure relaxes. Shortly before we wake, however, the body begins preparing for the day. Adrenaline, cortisol, blood pressure, and heart rate begin to rise. We literally hit the deck running. While we sleep, most of our muscles remain somewhat paralyzed while our eye muscles move back and forth. For unclear reasons men get repeated erections throughout the night. Some people will wake temporarily paralyzed (and panicked), as if a portion of the waking mechanism was delayed. Breathing remains intact, however, and this frightful state only lasts a few seconds.

Despite seeming so vulnerable during sleep, we are surprisingly protected. Very few of us fall out of bed, linger in one position too long and get bedsores, or smother in our pillows. Our body senses most problems early and automatically makes us change positions or move our head. We automatically kick the covers off when it's too hot or pull them up when we're chilled. If we're hurting from an old back injury in one position, we can roll to the other side without waking. Our ears are always listening. Our skin is like a home security system—a single out-of-the-ordinary touch and we awake.

Our physiology adjusts as well. Our kidneys slow their work so we don't have to get up every two hours. Our bowels slow down. Our saliva dries so we won't choke. Our eyeballs roll upward when we close our eyes, presumably for additional protection. Debris in our eyes is washed from the upper outer corners toward the lower inner corners and our eyes are kept lubricated at all times. Our mouth will function as a backup opening for breathing should our nostrils become plugged. We toss and turn so our muscles will not be stiff in the morning.

And it's not just us who are kept safe. Baboons sleep near tops of trees to avoid predators and do not fall out. Birds can perch and not fall over as they sleep. Bats do not drop from the tops of caves by the millions every day. Australian koala bears spend most of their lives sleeping in eucalyptus trees without dropping. Orcas can stay afloat for hours while asleep.

INSECTS

Insects have a sleeplike condition called *diapause,* which helps them withstand unfavorable conditions. Typically diapause happens in the winter, but this type of suspended animation can also happen when temperatures are too high or the climate too dry, quarters are cramped by overpopulation, or carbon dioxide levels have risen. It can also happen for reasons we've yet to discover.

The queen of a paper-wasp nest will chew a hole into an old tree trunk and sleep inside through the winter. Grasshoppers and butterflies might roll up inside a leaf. Bumblebees, ladybugs, and earwigs will lodge in wooden holes for the winter. The Colorado beetle, known for destroying crops, will sleep underground until the right moment.

Many insects have diapause hormones that are released when day length increases or soil temperature rises to needed levels. A tick will remain in dormancy until it gets a whiff of butyric acid arising from the sebaceous glands on a passing mammal. It suddenly comes to life, jumps on board, and digs in for a blood meal and a place to leave its eggs. The longest known "sleeping" tick was 18 years in a laboratory. One would guess there were no passing sebaceous glands.

■ ■ ■ ■

Every living being sleeps in some fashion. Most rest for minutes to hours, but some slumber for months, and a few even remain dormant for years. Sleep is critical, but the reasons why are not entirely clear. Without it, however, humans would die. (This fact has been proven by observation of families who have a genetic predisposition to insomnia.) Even though the instructions controlling sleep can be found within the DNA in every living cell, Darwinists have not been able to explain how restorative slumber came about. In fact, they avoid the topic. Rest assured, sleeping is not the result of an accident or mutation.

20. ADAPTATION

"You can be the most beautiful fish
that ever swam. You can be perfectly
equipped to survive. Then, one day
the pond you live in dries up, and that's
it, you die no matter how fit you are."

—STEPHEN JAY GOULD

Most animals and plants have an incredible array of adaptive skills. Those who cannot adapt have moved on to better pastures or died off. Perhaps that is why dinosaurs no longer exist. No one knows. Thousands of species have come and gone and the reasons for most are not clear.

Some species have clearly benefited from survival of the fittest (a true phenomenon), but they have to be variations on the genetic blueprint. It has to be written in the genetic code how this bird can grow a longer beak or that lizard can change to another color. Just needing better padding on the bottom of one's paws doesn't mean its offspring will just start having thicker soles. To change the padding on an animal's paws there would have to be additional genetic changes that correctly affect the circulation, the musculature, the regeneration or repair process, the color, the temperature, the texture, the durability, and many other aspects.

Beneficial mutations are exceedingly rare. Most mutations are minuscule or undetectable, or repaired; a few are devastating. Envision a crowded football stadium and 50,000 plus people holding up a red square. Then, on a signal, they turn it over, and the entire stadium becomes a sea of green colors. A mutation would be one person dropping their card.

The vast majority of living beings live within the temperate zones. Select species are designed to survive the intense heat of the tropics, where the temperature can exceed 120° F, the dryness of the desert where humidity approaches zero, or the frozen Arctic where temperatures may go below -50° F. Certain species can survive altitudes of five miles where oxygen tension is especially low. There are worms thriving miles beneath the ocean's surface where the pressure would readily crush a person. An ancient bacteria, called methanogens, reside miles beneath the earth's surface; and there are bacteria called anaerobes that live and work for us within our intestines without a need for oxygen.

Huskies retain heat by constricting blood vessels in their legs. Ducks standing on icy ponds restrict blood flow to their feet. Whales and seals are protected from the cold by blubber; arctic birds have extra feathers. Tropical birds use their wings for air conditioning. Musk oxen carry large deposits of brown fat inside their abdomen to maintain warm internal temperatures.

Certain snakes will regurgitate undigested food if the temperature suddenly drops, preventing the meal from decaying on the inside. Animals in the polar regions know how to utilize frozen water, and those in arid climates know how to maximize water retention.

Elephants and jack-rabbits lose heat through dilated blood vessels in their giant ears. Snails come out when times are wet and drink through their skin. During dry times they will close off the entrance to their shell with a film of mucus

Mutations—A Source of Disorder?

According to Michael Gross, author of *Life on the Edge*, "A living organism is something extremely improbable, and not only because you hardly find any in the universe at large. Mainly it is improbable because it represents a highly complicated, ordered structure, while the fundamental laws of thermodynamics (the science of energy conversions) tell us that the disorder of the universe (or any closed system) must increase with time."

or slime. Many fish who keep a swim bladder filled with variable amounts of air to control their buoyancy use the withheld oxygen when they sleep.

During the Hurricane Katrina floods in New Orleans, fire ants, which are essentially wingless wasps, balled up in huge groups that trapped air, like a porous beach ball, so they could float and roll on top of the moving water. Once the ball hit a tree or a house, they were ready to disengage and set up housekeeping.

Humans adapt in many ways, also. Aside from the obvious going to the movies or mall to cool off or throwing an extra log on the fire to warm up, we shiver to generate heat when we're cold and we sweat to lose heat when we're hot. Our heart rate and blood pressure increase when there are increased demands on our body, and they lessen when we rest. Our breathing rate increases when we need more oxygen, and our red blood cell production increases when we move to high altitudes that have lower oxygen concentrations. We grow protective calluses on our hands and feet when skin is exposed to trauma, and we tan in the sunlight to lessen future burning. Some of us store fat for hard times; some folks store fat for any reason.

The polar bear has an interesting mix of adaptive strategies that strongly point toward Design. Just its white color is a prime example. Black would seem better for living in freezing temperatures. It holds heat better. That's why we wear light colors in the summer and darker ones in the winter. But if its coat were black, the bears would not blend in with the ice floes and seals could more easily spot them. To make this conundrum work, Nature has made their pelts of hollow white hairs that trap heat and then channel it down to their black skin which absorbs it.

By contrast, camels survive incredibly high temperatures by allowing their body temperature to go up higher than most mammals and then storing the heat. Rather than sweating off the liters of fluid they need, they dissipate the heat at night, sometimes dropping their internal temperature by 7° C. When it comes to heat tolerance, however, the oryx, a Saharan antelope, puts the camel to shame. It hardly ever drinks and can tolerate a body temperature of 45° C (ours is 37° C). This temperature would fry other mammalian brains, but the oryx has a specialized network of blood vessels that protect its brain.

Try to calculate how many evolutionary steps would be needed to change a heat intolerant animal into a camel, taking into account all cellular needs and all changes in physiology. You can't, and scientists can't either.

21. CAMOUFLAGE

"Common sense is not so common."

—Voltaire

While our children play the game hide-and-seek only for fun, most other species engage in similar tactics for survival. The desire and wherewithal to do this is part of the whole package at conception. Continuance of the species and survival are the endgame, and camouflage is a skill that is particularly important if you're not the biggest, ugliest, toughest, fastest, smelliest, most poisonous, or meanest kid on the block. A rhinoceros needn't hide, but a cricket must. According to Bruce Purser, author of *Jungle Bugs: Masters of Camouflage and Mimicry,* "In our search for understanding of the natural world, we often inject a fairly massive dose of imagination into the process. Admirable as this may be, there is little guarantee that nature obeys the logic of humans."

■■■■■

Camouflage comes in two basic forms, passive and active. Both are preprogrammed; both can be illusions.

The passive version has more to do with overall appearance than instinctual behavior. It includes such things as size, shape, coloring, scent, and hangouts. Certain dark or speckled moths favor specific tree bark. Some insects grow up looking exactly like a diseased or

Hidden Plans

Humans make use of physical and psychological camouflage on a regular basis. Instead of planting a garden on our backs, we wear different clothes to fit in with a certain crowd or stand out. We cut, color, and style our hair to accomplish similar ends. We cover our odors with flower scents and our skin with makeup. We commonly camouflage our feelings as well. There's nothing like a smile and a pleasant comment. Sexual predators are particularly adept at camouflaging their intentions and their appearances. Military combatants are very well acquainted with camouflage. Reporters sometimes camouflage their personal agendas in the way they report the facts.

dying leaf, which is unappealing to both carnivores and herbivores. There's a bloblike caterpillar that has the unappetizing shape and color of bird excrement. Many fish have a darker back to resemble water from above and a lighter underside to resemble surface light. Certain butterflies are nearly transparent, looking like flowers from above and the sky from below. There's an invisible catfish in the tropics. There are flies that look like bees, moths that look like wasps, and frogs that look like cow patties. Seadragons in southern Australia look more like seaweed than sea horses.

The active version of camouflage incorporates a purposeful component. For example, the hognose snake flips over and plays dead when feeling threatened. This often works because most predators prefer their meals moving and alive. Flies and vultures don't show up because they already know it's a trick. The mere ability to lie motionless like the pit viper is a camouflage. A New Guinea weevil carries a deceptive garden on its back. When stationary, it looks like a tiny divot. It's not known whether this creature does the planting or these creatures have a purposefully attractive back for select plants. It works, nonetheless.

▪ ▪ ▪ ▪ ▪

A well-known expert at camouflage is the chameleon. Contrary to popular thought, this lizard does not change its color based on its surroundings. It already resembles the trees and plants where it resides. Instead, it changes colors based on heat, light, and temperament. Warning: Never mess with a chameleon that's changing to red and yellow. He's angry. If he's changing from brown to purple to blue and his eyelids are turning yellow with green spots, he's a little safer. Yet be careful, he's trying to attract a female chameleon, and he's not attracted to you. Chameleons make these changes by expanding and shrinking millions of specifically colored skin cells. It can be likened to the opening and closing of multicolored Venetian blinds.

This phenomenon is not explained by the theory of evolution. Indeed, one is hard put to find a discussion of it in any text. It is an all-or-none phenomenon. A partially concealed lizard would likely be very vulnerable.

Some animals don't need camouflage. The Komodo dragon for one has no predators. T. rex probably fell into a similar category. Some animals, like puffer fish, certain owls, and the horned toad, puff themselves up to look bigger and more intimidating. Some species, especially amphibians and certain reptiles, display Nature's brilliant warning colors, typically bright reds, oranges, or yellows, which tell predators they are poisonous or, at the least, will make them ill. The brightly colored poison-arrow frog is a prime example. In some way, this resembles our warnings such as the skull and crossbones or bottles with poisonous substances and the biohazard markings on containers of contaminated body fluids.

Camouflage comes into play when other species mimic a dangerous species. The nonpoisonous viceroy butterfly looks like the toxic monarch butterfly and thereby gains a survival benefit. A sphinx moth caterpillar moves like a snake. The jumping spider looks like unpalatable ants. The benign doppelgänger snake has the same stripes as the poisonous Brazilian coral snake.

Other incredible camouflages include that of the peacock flounder, which can blend in by mimicking the sandy, rocky terrain of the sea bottom in seconds. It actually changes its dorsal surface; it can even duplicate a checkerboard if placed on one in an aquarium. The case-bearing moth will weave a personal, body-length protective sweater from the materials in a garment it is presently eating. The dressing crab and many aquatic insects will cover their exoskeleton with debris from its surroundings. The tawny frogmouth looks identical to a stump of wood covered with lichen. The sargassum fish looks exactly like a sargassum floating weed. There are a lot of insects and amphibians with giant false eyes. Could they have tried smaller eyes before or single eyes? Not likely. The hairstreak butterfly has a false face at the wrong end.

■■■■■

It is readily apparent that simple colors play an important role in survival. Polar bears and Arctic foxes need to be white in order to survive among snowlands. Desert animals like the fennec (a type of fox) and many reptiles have to take on brown hues. Vine snakes need to be green. Female birds need to be drably colored to blend in with their nest and males colorful, perhaps to attract predators away from the nest.

For the most part, fossils tell us only about bones, teeth, beaks, eggs, and waste. They give us some perspective on time, but finding 65-million-year-old fossils on the surface in Montana, in the mountains in Alberta, Canada, and under tons of sediment in the Grand Canyon confuses the issues. Fossils don't tell us whether lizards or their predecessors were always green, or if sandy-colored animals always hung out at sandy-colored plots. Were they green originally and rather than changing, steadily shifted to greener parts? No one truly knows. Fossils tell us practically nothing about camouflage.

The question comes up, could these protective colors, shapes, or styles have evolved gradually by the laws regarding survival of the fittest? If the genes will only allow a species to become a certain intensity or shade of green and no darker, despite survival of the fittest, there has to be a very precise, coincidental mutation at the time it is needed, that can also be passed on. If this species needs to become more green through the millennia, there have to be recurring, precise, and timed mutations affecting very specific anatomy and physiology. It seems impossible.

22. TEMPERATURE REGULATION

"The temperature range for animal life is very narrow compared to cosmic temperatures, but nonetheless, suitable temperatures can be found throughout the oceans and over much of the surface of the earth, at least for part of the year."

—KNUT SCHMIDT-NIELSEN,
PROFESSOR OF PHYSIOLOGY, DUKE UNIVERSITY
AUTHOR OF **ANIMAL PHYSIOLOGY**

Although there are some odd exceptions, most species can be categorized as cold-blooded or warm-blooded. The cold-blooded group depends entirely on its environment for temperature and includes nearly every creature in the sea except whales and similar mammals, as well as reptiles, amphibians, and insects. The warm-blooded group is mostly mammals and birds. Both groups require very different temperature maintenance programs.

To transition from one to another, as evolutionary theory assumes, might be like moving the city of Anchorage, Alaska, to the Panama Canal and making simultaneous changes in everyone's clothing, housing, heating systems, hobbies, and eating habits. Jobs would change; sleeping patterns would be altered. There would even be new diseases.

■ ■ ■ ■ ■

Temperature control, which is also called thermoregulation, in humans requires an incredible list of interactions between several organ systems, customized hormonal changes from minute to minute, varied uses of select proteins and sugars, alternating routes in blood flow, closely monitored salt and fluid balances, varied use of millions of sweat glands, control mechanisms for heart rate and blood pressure, behavior modifications, cooperation between trillions of individual cells, and linkage between hundreds of mitochondria (biological batteries) within each cell. Having a 24/7 system that maintains each of us at 98.6° F, or 37.0° C (range 96.0° F /35.5° C to 104° F/40° C) is an incredible piece of physiology.

An internal temperature of 98.6° F, or 37.0° C, is only an average, however, based on a study done decades ago. Each person's true temperature varies with time of day, type of meal, age, level of emotion, degree of activity, certain medications, fatigue, and illness. Testicles are kept cooler for more efficient sperm production (an accident?). If there's an infection, the body will automatically raise its temperature, purposefully causing a fever, to fight the invaders. The brain is kept slightly warmer for, it's presumed, better thinking; and although our skin temperature may change based on the climate, we have a fatty layer beneath the skin's surface that functions as an internal insulation. It is similar to whale's blubber.

COLD-BLOODED TO WARM-BLOODED?

Most Darwinists say all life began in the sea. Since most large bodies of water in the temperate regions tend to stay within a narrow range of temperature, the lack of internal regulation was not a priority early on. The transition to land, however, brought different requirements. Outdoor temperatures can vary rather widely. On freezing days, cold-blooded species remain cold and somewhat listless; on warmer days, they can get about rather easily. Extremes force all of them to stay put.

To help mitigate this problem, some cold-blooded species change the color of their skin to absorb or reflect light differently, shift their position showing a less vulnerable side to the sun, or spread their extremities out to maximize heat absorption. The evolutionary downside is that cold-blooded animals need some amount of sunlight every morning. If the theory of evolution is correct and only cold-blooded animals populated the world for millions of years, there may have been extended days to years when nothing "alive" was moving.

The fossil record is not at all clear when warm-blooded species showed up on Earth. Theories depend, in part, on whether one believes that dinosaurs were cold-blooded or not. Until recently, the general consensus was that they were cold-blooded—giant lizards of sorts—but there is increasing evidence they may have actually not been. After all, how could a 20-ton animal warm up every morning?

Bone structures within fossilized dinosaurs resemble those of warm-blooded animals much more than cold-blooded animals, as we know them. A dinosaur's posture of standing upright on all fours and its way of walking resembles land mammals much more than reptiles whose legs are stretched out from the sides. And mammals may have already appeared by that time. Very recent findings in China show that *Gobicodon zofiae,* a rat-sized mammal, lived among these presumed reptiles.

A few folks on the fringe even claim to have found fossilized human footprints lying next to dinosaur footprints.

WARMING UP

Many of the "newer" warm-blooded animals do not have to hibernate for the winter or migrate thousands of miles. They can even hunt on a cold night. Because they have higher and dependable temperatures, they have more efficient hearts, better brains, more speed, and a better chance to survive any cataclysmic climate changes.

The bigger the animal, the less relative surface to lose heat. An elephant can handle temperature changes better than a hummingbird, whose maximum heart rate can go up to an incredible *1200* beats per minute. The rate of heat production must equal the rate of heat loss. Warm-blooded animals have some variability in their core temperatures, but for the most part they remain between 86° and 106° F, or 30° and 41° C (mammals at 36° to 38°, monotremes, like the platypus, at 30° to 31°, marsupials at 36° to 38°, and birds at 39 to 41°).

Assuming that being warm-blooded is an evolutionary advancement, increased survival benefits among the newer species seem like strong arguments for the theory of evolution. There are, however, way too many unexplained steps (links) between cold- and warm-blooded species.

When we sweat, which is a complex, coordinated process, evaporation cools us. The stronger the breeze or the drier the ambient climate, the more quickly we cool. When our blood vessels dilate (another huge coordinated process), cooler air takes on some of that heat by convection. If we stand close to a fireplace, conduction carries the heat internally; if we step into a cold room, the heat moves externally. When we breathe in cool air, our labyrinth-like sinuses warm it up for the body to use, again by conduction. Despite being sound asleep, we will automatically kick the covers off if we are too hot. We will also, automatically, shiver to produce heat.

Shivering appears to be unique to warm-blooded animals. The only known cold-blooded animal that can raise its temperature by muscle contraction is the python, but this is more by rhythmic muscle contractions during digestion and brooding eggs. Baldness versus hairiness and ear size play a role. Elephants lose heat through complex superficial blood vessels in giant ears, whereas the furry mammoth had tiny ears.

RANGES AND TOLERANCES

There is a very wide range of temperature tolerances and accommodations within the animal kingdom and very few explanations of how they even came about. Many birds and mammals can increase their heat production tenfold. Mammals can move their huge bodies in ways that would exhaust a cold-blooded animal. Polar bears can swim hundreds of kilometers amidst ice floes, and killer whales can hunt among ice packs without ill effects. A husky's body temperature is 38° C while its paws remain near zero to minimize heat loss (when out on the snow) or injury. A large number of insects, worms, and bacteria can live at near-freezing temperatures without significant fat storage.

The spring peeper *(Pseudacris crucifer)*, a North American frog, can survive up to three days with half of its body frozen. Polar fish have an antifreeze protein called glycoprotein that prevents ice crystals from forming inside their bodies. The Alaska blackfish *(Dallia pectorallis)* can actually be supercooled to -4° F (-20° C) for 30 minutes and survive. Certain types of algae normally grow (bloom) on ice. And the midge chironomus can be repeatedly frozen and thawed without harm.

At the other end of the spectrum are the heat-tolerant species. The Devil's Hole pupfish can live in hot springs in excess of 93.2° F (33.9° C). A small crab in Tunisia survives in water at 97.5° to 117.5° F (36.5° to 47.5° C). Six-feet-tall worms found standing beside hydrothermal vents deep in the Pacific near the Galápagos Islands withstand temperatures up to 176° F (80° C). Dr. Karl P.N. Shuker likens this to sitting on a hot plate. That notwithstanding, there are microbes that can withstand autoclaving for an hour at 250° F.

There are some mixed cases, also. Tunas, billfishes, and lamnid sharks keep some of their muscles warmer than the rest of their body, the so-called regionally warm-blooded species. This did not "evolve" for walking onto land, but it's more for diving into deeper, colder water and swimming faster than prey. Certain insects including moths, beetles, and bees are warm-blooded when they are flying. Their flight muscles must be warmed up in advance; if the weather is too cold, they may not be able to fly.

An oddity among mammals is the naked mole rat, an African subterranean animal; it lives like termites and has no temperature regulation. It is a cold-blooded mammal whose internal temperatures are precisely that of the ground around it.

■ ■ ■ ■ ■

So, how did it happen? For the theory of evolution to be correct, there had to have been a near-infinite number of changes in the brain and circulatory system affecting billions of cells.

The transition from cold-blooded species to warm-blooded species is enormous and there is no clear evidence any lukewarm-blooded transition species ever existed.

If one were using the chain-link fence analogy, the gate is missing.

PART FIVE
IMPROBABLE NATURAL INSTINCTS

> "The very essence of an instinct is that it
> is followed independently of reason."
>
> —CHARLES DARWIN

Instincts are the unlearned behaviors that are automatically passed from generation to generation. They help keep all species safe, healthy, warm or cool, hydrated, nourished, and reproducing. These capabilities are often taken for granted, as if this task were simply accomplished with the wanting, yet each one is extremely complex, well-coordinated, deeply rooted, distinctly purposeful, rarely wavering, and incredibly unique. Although most are directly geared toward survival, a few may not be. Most help guide every species through daily activities such as hunting, fighting, defending themselves, their home, or their group, homemaking, foraging, playing, birthing, parenting, and hiding.

Humans like to think that we have freed ourselves of our instinctual behavior. Indeed, some of us pride ourselves on rising above animal behaviors, but for the most part, we're fooling ourselves. Our instincts are constantly working for us at home, play and work, every day of our lives. What attracts you to your spouse? What tells you a dark alley isn't safe? How do you know water or food is not safe?

The knowledge that a chick has on how and when to break out of an egg has to be preprogrammed. Nothing else makes sense. The knowledge used by baby scorpions to climb onto their mother's back for safety, by a baby giraffe to stand up, by a puppy to nurse,

or a kangaroo to hide inside its mom's pouch are all inherited pro-
gramming (instincts). How does a newborn robin know not to step
beyond the boundary of its nest? And when it's finally okay to do
so?

Could a human baby's cry be there purposely to tell its parents
something's gone awry? Where would the newborn have learned this
skill? Certainly not in utero. Crying is not a simple process either.
It involves recognizing a pressing need such as pain, hunger, thirst,
or discomfort, then it requires the anatomical ability to coordinate
billions of cells in the brain, lungs, chest wall, neck, and voicebox
to turn on the right emotion, and eventually requires the ability to
turn the crying off once the need is satisfied. Imagine how it might
be if any newborn species felt hunger yet lacked a way to express
the need.

■ ■ ■ ■ ■

Naturalists and scientists have argued for centuries whether
some components of animal behavior might be conscious decision-
making. Some of us like to think we are the only animals that think
(human chauvinism?), but there is increasing anecdotal evidence to
the contrary. Pet owners are certain their pets make decisions and
even try to communicate.

Crisis-response dogs seem to know when comforting is needed.
Laboratory animals have been seen to cry when researchers approach
them. Gorillas have been photographed using broken tree limbs to
test the depth of the water while crossing a river. One female gorilla
at the Bronx Zoo reportedly saved a three-year-old child who had
fallen into her pen from the other gorillas and then handed the child
to her mother through the iron bars. Orangutans will pick open a
lock on their cage after the staff has gone home for the night. Octopi
will hide a pilfered item with a single tentacle while maintaining
direct eye contact with their caretakers. Skunks will pound their
feet before making the decision to spray. Even a rattlesnake may
make a conscious decision to inject venom with their bite. Not all

bites include their deadly poison. No one knows how or why that happens. Burrowing owls will present themselves to an intruder with wings spread wide, and the young make a "rattlesnake rasp" sound if threatened. This is why legends say they share their nests with rattlesnakes.

Virtually every aspect of animal behavior can be directly or indirectly linked to instincts. Following are some of the more commonly discussed areas.

23. HOME-BUILDING

"A man's home is his wife's castle."

— HENNY YOUNGMAN

Whether it be a burrow, den, nest, or a lair, home-building is a good example of instinctual behavior. Some homes are incredibly intricate. All birds seem to know which structural elements are needed and where to find them, where to best set up or find their home, how to secure it, when to start work, when to stop, what types of foliage will discourage insect pests, how to knit the components together, how best to camouflage it, and how to defend it. They are born with these instincts.

Deftly coordinating his beak and feet, a male weaver bird will build an incredibly sturdy hanging nest. It begins as a perch hung from a forked twig and evolves into a complex piñata-like sphere of interwoven strips of vegetation secured by many tight knots. An African weaver builds a skyscraper version. Its nest can reach 12 by 3 by 3 feet and may contain as many as 150 separate bedrooms.

No one knows what component of this ability, if any, is maternal instruction early on, or whether perhaps the baby birds memorize their architectural surroundings, but a very large percentage seems to be inborn. Generation after generation has the uncanny ability to construct marvelously intricate nests that are recognizably their style.

One might ask, could nest building have evolved by tiny, evolutionary steps (links)? Did the early birds collect random twigs,

Weaver birds construct a complex interwoven and intricate nest for their family. No one has ever shown that this ability developed in steps over a series of generations.

© Nigel J. Dennis / Photo Researchers, Inc.[7]

perhaps for the fun of it, and then some clever bird recognize the advantage of putting a few together? Did he or she then pass this useless information on until one of the grandchildren had the brilliant idea to make a nest? Suppose your parents were both fantastic magicians and you had watched them all through your childhood cutting a beautiful woman in half. This skill, which you might master as well, will never become part of your genetic makeup, no matter how profitable. As far as we know it cannot change to cellular DNA. So how did nest-making make it there?

■ ■ ■ ■ ■

There are many unique and interesting homes in nature. Termites build huge domelike structures that have their own climate control. Anthills contain their own dump sites and gardens. Every night the parrot fish secretes transparent mucus that forms an all-encompassing, jellylike cocoon. This gooey sleeping bag masks its odor and protects it from predators. Half of a gooey cocoon (an intermediary step or link) won't do the job. The European water spider makes its own diving bell by spinning a silken sheet that she attaches to nearby plants, then carries individual bubbles of air from the surface to tap inside this underwater umbrella. The aquatic larva of the caddis fly builds a tightly fitting tubular home of twigs, pebbles, and debris that prevents fish from swallowing it.

The potter wasp makes a mud nest that resembles an inverted vase. If the mud is too dry she will moisten it with her own saliva; if too wet, she will wait until it dries. After her home is completed, she captures a caterpillar or other unlucky insect, forces it into the vase, lays an egg inside, and seals the nest off. Once the newborn hatches, it knows to kill and eat the captive insect.

A queen paper wasp makes her preliminary home of hexagonal cells with chewed wood mixed with saliva. Once a few workers have hatched, they take over building a much larger papier-mâché home of the same chewed products.

The male Australian incubator bird, or moundbuilder, builds

a mound 20 feet across, 50 feet high, and 6 feet underground, which maintains its eggs at precisely 91° F and 99 percent humidity. The parents make absolutely sure these parameters are met and maintained. Newborns breathe through cone-shaped pores in their eggs and shave off the tapered, smaller ends as they age so that the hole gets larger as their needs increase. This behavior is not taught. Somehow, after the offspring is born, it also knows how to dig out and immediately forage for itself. Eventually it too will build another mound when mating, without any how-to books.

Burrowing is another curious home-making style. The hairy armadillo, or pichiciegos, has armored-plated buttocks, which it uses to lock the entrance to its burrow. The shield-tail agama from the Somalia desert has a similar defense. This is a four-inch-long lizard with a wide, spiny tail that it uses to block the entrance to its burrow at night.

Moles make burrows their entire way of life. And contrary to popular opinion, all moles are not alike. The golden mole is related to elephants, albeit much smaller, and the marsupial mole is related to kangaroos. The naked mole-rat is actually a rodent, and it runs its life more like an insect than a mammal, forming colonies and adopting a king and queen. Royalty make their servants drink their hormone-laden urine so that the lesser citizens will not be interested in reproduction. One wonders how that evolved. Entryways to burrows are often camouflaged, and back-door escape routes are not uncommon. Sometimes there are many escape routes.

A WEB OF MARVELS

The making of a spider's web is also species-specific and instinctual. Strand for strand, their silk threads are stronger than steel, yet they can also stretch 25 percent. Steel cannot. These fibers begin as a complex proteinaceous liquid, oozing through internal pathways, that is secreted through spinnerets near the rear end of the insect. It hardens immediately as it is being laid down. Imagine how it might be if, in evolution terms, the original silk took hours to solidify or there was only one spinneret. Chaotic, slumping webs would be ineffective, to say the least. All of these webs had to have been done correctly from the start.

Although the patterns, shapes, and sizes of most spiderwebs are species-specific, there are some variations. The black and yellow garden spider has at least seven kinds of webbing. Webs can include up to 65 feet of silk with as many as 1000 junctions. Many arachnids will build from the inside out, and they seem to know exactly how much silk fluid is available to be used. Humans call this planning ahead, but this stuff is preprogrammed.

▪▪ SPIDER SPINNERETS ▪▪

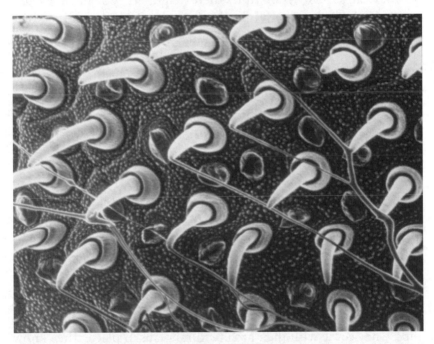

Using very specifically constructed and complicated mechanisms, spiders secrete sticky silk threads from ducts on their spinnerets. These quickly harden into strands that are put together in specific patterns, depending on whether a web, cocoon, or trip line is being produced. The theory of evolution has not offered a wisp of any intermediate type of web.

© David Scharf / Photo Researchers, Inc.[8]

The orb spider will make a pentagon-shaped web, starting with an upper horizontal thread, then dropping straight down from the middle with a vertical thread, adding radial threads to nearby structures for support, and finishing with outwardly swirling, interwoven sticky thread. The strongest web fiber known comes from nephilia spiders in the South Sea Islands. It is used to make fishnets.

Spiders can make horizontal sticky strands with vertical nonsticky ones or have multiple locations studded with globs of glue. They know how or where to walk. Imagine how long this species would have lasted if they kept getting stuck in their own web. Some have draglines for quick escapes. Many webs weigh less than a milligram, yet they can support 4000 times their weight. They swing like hammocks and act like dozens of sticky bungee cords when struck by a flying insect. An added design includes the fact that the more the insect struggles, the more it becomes ensnared. The spider, sensing the motion, hurries to the scene and quickly wraps her captive in more thread while injecting its venom. Many spiders will then regurgitate stomach enzymes, which externally digest the victim. They then suck the juices out at their leisure.

■ ■ ■ ■ ■

If you were to build your own home, what would be your priorities? Protection from the elements? Creature comforts? Enough space? A strategic location? Easy access? Attractiveness? Distance from intrusive neighbors? Sturdiness? Enough storage space? Room for kids? Adequate plumbing, ventilation, and electrical outputs?

You can request these and, given the finances, get what you want. Animals don't need to study home plans and get competitive bids. They come with their architectural plans in place. They know where to find the building materials, and they know where and how to place them. If they didn't come with this blueprint, how many generations of burrowing animals would have survived before their roofs stopped caving in? Anything short of an entire, complete Design might terminate the species.

24. DEFENSE AND OFFENSE

"Ignorant people think it's the noise which fighting cats make that's so aggravating, but it ain't so; it's the sickening grammar they use."

— MARK TWAIN

Defensive and offensive skills are driven primarily by instincts. They can be automatic or calculated, proactive or reactive, and sometimes accomplished in milliseconds. They are geared toward survival; this clearly is the "eat or be eaten" philosophy. Yet there is little time to learn and practice survival techniques. Predators are usually nearby and waiting. Granted, a few offspring may briefly observe their parents' behaviors, but overall most species spend relatively little time with their parents. Some never even meet them, yet they seem to know everything they need to know.

Evolutionary science cannot explain how any survival skills came about. It's not likely that they merely appeared on their own. And just because a brand new, protective maneuver worked once, doesn't mean it would be passed on to other generations. In fact, it could have worked several times and it still would not have been inherited. It would have to be taught to each new generation. In addition, there has to be a mechanism to recognize something new that worked and a way to remember or store it.

All living beings have to instinctively know the whens, whats, whys, wheres, and hows of survival. This is a biological, genetic book of instructions that every species passes along in their genes.

Some need species-specific maternal input; some never get maternal input.

■ ■ ■ ■ ■

Two faced-off, growling dogs or two bucks with locked antlers are simple examples of offensive and defensive maneuvers. There's an incredible array of fascinating and unexplained skills. Every one of them depends on the coordination of millions of complex chemicals and billions of cellular interactions. Every living being needs a way to detect an intruder, recognize whether it is friend or foe, and then decide whether to issue a warning, retreat, or go into attack mode. How useful is a deaf watchdog?

CHEMICAL WARFARE

Chemical warfare is one type of instinctual behavior, particularly in the insect and plant world. Although most species use chemicals purely for defense, a few species like ants bite first and then spray the wound with pain-inducing formic acid. Arthropods spray, spit, wear, defecate, regurgitate, ooze, salivate, release, and even exude very irritating and sometimes poisonous substances that somehow have remained harmless while harbored in their bodies.

Science does not yet know how the whip scorpion can store a poison which is 84 percent acetic acid without dissolving itself. One would think that the manufacturing process would cause self-destruction. This acid is housed in two anal glands and, by design, it has 5 percent caprylic acid, a fat solvent, to help dissolve the waxy exoskeleton of the scorpion's prey. That way the acid can do even more damage.

The sawfly larva can store a mixed repellent and poison (1,8-cineole, beta-phellandrene, piperone, and other poisons from aldehydes, alcohols, and phenols taken from eucalyptus leaves) inside a lined cavity or pouch in its throat. When attacked, these larvae circle around like covered wagons and then collectively regurgitate the nasty stuff. As soon as the predator has departed, they re-ingest the same nasty oils and store them in the same pouches. There are countless missing links to this behavior alone.

The millipede uses a tranquilizer similar to quaalude—an older sleeping medication. Obviously, the sedating chemical doesn't help the individual millipede who has been eaten, but it puts the predator to sleep. It becomes vulnerable to predation, which protects the remaining millipedes.

The honeybee stinger emits a pheromone that attracts fellow bees to join the fight. In a similar manner, many ants will secrete an alarm pheromone, along with formic acid, that attracts extremely zealous reinforcements.

An Australian termite called the nasui termite acts like a combination suicide bomber and artillery unit. If provoked by a predator, it will swing its head side to side and squirt loops of a chemical mix. One component will glue the attacker in place, another will paralyze it, another may kill it, and a fourth will attract other termite soldiers to gather around the intruder and keep spraying it. Their sprays contain alpha-pinene, beta-pinene, limonene, trinervitrenes, and kempanes. The latter two chemicals cause the stickiness, and they have not been found anywhere else in nature. This species also defies evolutionary logic.

Beetle species are especially known for squirting noxious chemicals at predators. They have an incredible selection of concoctions that are stored in special glands found in antennae, heads, flanks, rear ends, all extremities, or a combination of locations. If one were to squeeze an extremity with a soft forceps, one would see a drop of poison exude from the nearest joint. Some insects will exude drops of poison from all extremities; others will exude them from pores along their flanks. The eleodes beetle, referred to as the skunk of the entomological world, has a feculent-smelling spray.

The bombardier beetle squirts two chemicals from separate rear-end nozzles that can be aimed in any direction. When these normally benign chemicals combine, they heat up and hit the opponent at the temperature of 100° C, causing a miniature explosion. The geophilid centipedes exude the highly poisonous hydrogen cyanide gas that quickly paralyzes their predators; yet they can carry this deadly poison around without any ill effects. Other millipedes can spray this poisonous gas as far as 30 centimeters, or two feet. The green lynx spider can spit venom from eight inches away. A whirligig beetle will release a foul secretion that will cause a largemouth bass to spit it back out.

▨▨ BOMBARDIER BEETLE ▨▨

This African insect squirts two different chemicals from separate cannons in its rear that, when combined, will burn and kill small predators. They can even burn people's eyes. The compounds are harmless in their separate storage chambers, but deadly together. The beetle can aim accurately and fire repeatedly.

The entire mechanism defies evolution. How and why would there have been a gradual development of chemicals that were useless until they finally reached their present form? This system is all or nothing.

© *Eye of Science / Photo Researchers, Inc.*[9]

Are these all merely lucky chemical mutations that protected the species? Why so many? Why not just one or two? And why so complicated? How did the special storage glands that protect the owner evolve? Before or after? Or at the same time?

What happened to the thousands of missing links?

Plant Chemicals

Altogether, worldwide, plants and mushrooms are estimated to have at least 100,000 different chemical weapons stored up and ready to use, or else they have the ingredients ready to be combined upon demand. Some have direct poisons or toxins, others have repellents or adhesives. They use chemicals to attract protectors and other chemicals to deter predators. They use chemical messages to warn each other of danger. Whenever spider mites infest bean plants, the bean plants send a chemical signal to carnivorous mites, which will kill the intruders.

Most of us know to avoid stinging nettles, poison oak, and poison ivy, but do you know that St. John's wort, a common, herbal anti-depressant, has a chemical defense that is very toxic to livestock and most insects? It is light-sensitive. If eaten during the day, sunlight impacts the chemical as it traverses through blood vessels in the skin and converts it into a toxin. Most herbivores instinctively know to avoid it.

Whenever the corn plant *Zea mays* is attacked by beet army worms, the saliva causes the plant to release a volatile signal that attracts the female *Cotesia marginniventris* wasp, which lays her eggs in these predators. As the wasp larvae hatch, they kill the army worms. The swollen thorn acacia tree secretes a sugary syrup to bribe ants into living in its hollow thorns and protecting it.

The Bolivian wild potato is one of the most resistant potato species. Its leaves are covered with tiny hairs that secrete a sticky substance. This adhesive not only slows the aphids and other predators down, but their further steps pull open glands on the leaf's surface that release very deadly chemicals.

Poison Everywhere

There are examples of chemical warfare within every species. The hagfish will slime its predator to death. The horned lizard can squirt blood out of its eyes, presumably scaring predators away. The chameleon has an optically guided sticky tongue missile. Certain moths will exude a foul-smelling poisonous foam when approached. A cobra can accurately spit venom eight feet, causing permanent blindness and severe pain. The shrew will attack animals several times its size and kill with a venom nearly identical to a cobra's venom. The death-feigning opossum will secrete a putrid oil from its rear end. The fulmar chick defends itself with projectile vomiting that can damage feathers. These chicks will sometimes surprise a weekend cliff-climber with reeking stomach oils as they peek their head over a ledge.

The skunk stands on its front legs, shifts its anus over its head, and lets an intruder have it. This spray can go several yards and typically causes instant vomiting. The champion of excrement warfare, however, may be the fieldfare bird. If they sense the presence of an intruder, such as a magpie, they

Cotton plants under attack will heighten their defensive chemical production and warn neighbor plants. Injured poplar trees will send a warning to other poplar trees, which will intensify their defenses. And the creosote bush not only makes several hundred volatile chemicals to discourage predators, but some of their chemicals prohibit other plants from growing nearby.

VARIATIONS ON THE THEME

The bristle millipede is covered with tiny tufts and rows of Velcro-like bristles that easily detach when the insect is attacked. There are hundreds of tiny hooks on these tufts which can tie two or more legs together. The harder an ant tries to escape the bristles, the more its extremities become permanently ensnared. The dead ant will soon look like a roped cow at a rodeo. The crested rat of North Africa, which resembles a skunk more than a rat, exudes a foul-smelling secretion along its flanks that has been known to kill attacking dogs.

The fire beast caterpillar looks like a miniature guinea pig, but this character has venomous spines hidden within the apparent fluff. Certain moths have detachable scales allowing them to easily escape spider webs; whiteflies are covered with wax that doesn't stick to spider webs; and green lacewings have special hairs on their wings that prevent them from sticking. Given enough time, the lacewing will slide down the web and merely fall off before flying away. Just in case the spider shows up too soon, it can also secrete a foul-smelling liquid.

The three-banded armadillo can roll up into an impenetrable ball. In like manner, so can a hedgehog. The echidna, who dines on ants and termites with its long snout and a sticky tongue, digs itself into a burrow, only leaving the sharp spines on its back visible.

will take to the air and collectively bombard it with blobs of sticky excrement that can destroy the waterproofing and insulation of feathers. While squawking about the attack, the magpie may even catch some of the feces in its mouth and leave the area gagging. These are aimed, not accidental hits. The fieldfare bird's bombing requires an enormous amount of instinctual calculation, which happens on the wing, to get the trajectory correct to hit another bird, which may also be moving.

The clown fish resides among the poisonous tentacles of the sea anemone and will actually be pulled inside if the anemone senses danger. In exchange it cleans the anemone and chases off predators. Poison-dart frogs obtain their poisons from their diet and then store specific chemicals in their skin for protection. Their bright colors serve as a warning that predators may get ill. Those who tempt fate, and survive, remember those colors forever. This frog is also covered with slime that makes it slippery to predators and contains antibiotics that protect it from the multitudes of bacteria commonly found in dirty ponds.

A large group of snails found in the South Pacific fire off venom-packed hollow darts at passing prey, which normally move a lot faster than they can. They use nerve toxins, called conotoxins, fired from the tip of their proboscis (nose). They are more poisonous than most snake venoms, and there have even been human deaths reported. These snails make use of hydrostatic pressure to launch their missiles and they can reload in less than ten minutes. To manufacture a paralyzing poison, house it securely, package it, and accurately fire it defies any stepwise explanation from evolution.

Certain lizards, upon sensing danger, are capable of detaching a portion of their tail as they take off. The wriggling body part will distract the predator long enough for the lizard to get away, and it also serves as a time-buying snack. This is a win-win scenario. Whenever or however this adaptation came about, it could not have been through a Darwinian mechanism like survival of the fittest. No matter how often or how severely an animal is mutilated, that change is not transferred to the genes, even if it might be beneficial.

OUT OF SIGHT

The microscopic world is loaded with various chemical defenses. One of the most commonly used antibiotics, penicillin, is a biological weapon. In 1928 a chance observation by Dr. Alexander Fleming ultimately saved many lives. He had noticed that the mold *Penicillium notatum,* which accidentally landed on his culture plates, secreted a toxin that killed microorganisms. Ten years later penicillin was isolated, purified, and prescribed as a miraculous antibiotic. This led to other searches, and soon streptomycin and neomycin were discovered in the streptomyces arsenal.

The bacteria species *E. fecalis* has one large chemical and one small chemical that travel together alongside the microorganism. If the large chemical attaches to an approaching cell (assumed intruder or predator), the small chemical breaks free and returns to the bacteria. That prompts the release of a very potent toxin that can also be very dangerous for humans.

Just like the battles in the jungle or forests, microorganisms battle with biological shields, armor, spears, hatchets, sprays, harpoons, and chemicals. No one has yet demonstrated a shouting match or name-calling, but who knows. They can hit and run, pursue, overwhelm, and hunt in groups. Some have intricate sensing capabilities. Some can change shape and size based on the needs of the moment. Some can change tactics midstream.

■■ BACTERIA ATTACKING WHITE CELL ■■

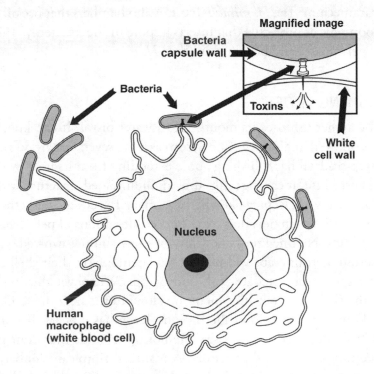

Magnified image

Bacteria capsule wall

Bacteria

Toxins

White cell wall

Nucleus

Human macrophage (white blood cell)

Bacteria like those causing typhoid fever inject complex paralyzing toxins into the host's macrophages (white blood cells), using an extremely complex syringe-and-needle system.

The chance that this came about by evolution is less likely than a non-Russian-speaking person stepping off a train in Moscow and finding their way to a hotel 20 miles away without a map or guide, or a means of transportation besides walking.

Illustration by Dana Csakany.

The paramecium has trichocysts, which are cannonlike structures with a toxic cannonball. They are extremely fast-moving for their environment and attack by firing a long, tough thread with a sticky barb. The paramecium's enemy is the *Didinium nauutum*. This organism comes with a long proboscis (nose) loaded with toxic trichocysts (torpedoes). The organism rams its proboscis like a battering ram into the paramecium, firing off these toxic cysts until the microorganism is paralyzed. It then opens its proboscis and swallows the paramecium. The *H. mirablis* has missile chambers that fire off a harpoon type of projectile that inserts a spore inside its enemy. This spore germinates and becomes another *H. mirablis.*

FINISHING IT OFF

The archer fish uses its mouth like a water pistol. It can knock insects off overhanging vegetation from as far as seven feet away. The wolftrap seadevil has a "fishing" pole extending from its head with a line and a lure. It can cast this lure, an illuminated structure with two hooks, toward its prey like a fly fisherman. The crested basketfish catches its dinner in nets that are supposed alterations of pelvic and pectoral fins. No one knows how any of these abilities evolved.

Certain hermit crabs will plant a sea anemone on their shell to protect them from predator fish and octopi. Whenever they out-grow the shell, they take the anemone along to the next one…like a pet Doberman. A crab in the Indian Ocean has pincers that are specifically designed to carry sea anemones. It holds them out in threatening ways toward predators. A mantis shrimp can clobber a small crab with a punch equivalent in force to a .22-caliber bullet, usually breaking through the shell. Given the opportunity, they can also break the glass in an aquarium. Another mantis shrimp can fire off a spear at enormous speeds to kill its prey. These shrimp have eyes that move independently and seem to see colors much more in depth than we can. No one has a clear idea how they came about.

The sea wasp is the deadliest jellyfish. It has enough venom to kill 60 humans and it can fire a barb in less than three milliseconds (a millisecond is a thousandth of a second). The toadfish carries one of the most venomous poisons known in its spines. A wrong step by a person could be a fatal mistake.

The bola spider makes a sticky, poisonous lasso that it throws at passing insects. Net-throwing spiders create a pheromone that attracts moths, and then they toss a silken net to capture them. One wonders how many nets were tried through the millennium until the right one worked. And of course, it can't be passed in the genes if it's a learned skill. Certain crab spiders look like flowers; when a curious insect lands, they merely grab hold of a meal. The fisher spider can stand on the surface of water and use one of its legs as a lure.

Several species of fungi that live deep in the soil are active hunters. These are another form of mushrooms. They can sense movement and this will prompt the release of a sticky substance that immobilizes their victim. As in a science-fiction movie, they send filaments into their victim and drain them dry of nutrients. One species of fungi has a three-cell lasso, which is triggered whenever a worm crawls through the loop. The cells immediately swell, capturing the worm, and then its interior is invaded by fungal filaments. Not a pretty sight, I'm sure.

Honeybees have a group function to defend their colonies and kill wasps. Two species, *Apis cerana* and *Apis mellifera,* will wrap an intruding wasp in a ball of as many as 6000 bees and cook them to death. Apparently, they can generate heat that exceeds the wasp's tolerance and yet will not injure them significantly. Otherwise, these wasps, which can have a wingspan of two-and-a-half inches, will attack a nest, kill every soldier insect one by one, and then steal the larva to feed their young.

■ ■ ■ ■ ■

Nature might be viewed as an endless canvas of three-dimensional chess games. Offense, defense, trickery. Every species has its own unique set of tools to capture food, fool predators, attack, retreat, and defend its family. All of these are intricate maneuvers that could not have evolved separately. If they had, a newer species might be destroyed by the experienced grand master every time.

25. REPRODUCTION

"I was so ugly when I was born, the doctor slapped my mother."

— RODNEY DANGERFIELD

Most scientists believe that the goal of every living being is to perpetuate its own species by nearly any means possible, but also under controlled and appropriate circumstances. Nearly every physiological function seems to be, in some way, directly or indirectly geared toward survival of the individual and survival of the species.

For most, reproduction takes place during specific times, in specific ways, and at specific places. There is no wasted effort or time. Man may be the only or one of very few exceptions. Nature cannot afford to have the male guessing when the eggs are ready for fertilization. There's food to be gotten, water to be found, and burrows to be dug. Many animals give birth in the spring. Is that an evolutionary accident or Design? Spring is so much more amenable to raising young than winter. It has to be in the genes. There is no scientific evidence to support alternative times for mating or trials that failed among ancient predecessors. Everything seems to have been arranged to maximize survival of offspring from the very start of life.

COURTING

Some female species send out signals announcing that they are fertile—*It's time to make babies, better hurry and find me.* These can be chemical, sonic, electrical, tactile, bioluminescent, or visual communications. Nearly every species has its own unique ways. Humans, in contrast, seem clueless without a thermometer and calendar; we procreate in a more random fashion. Perhaps we were designed to enjoy the sexual act more. Few animals are as sexually active as we. For them, mating is accomplished like hunting, just another function of life. So it seems.

The male Indian moon moth can detect a female's pheromones from three miles away. As he approaches her, he will leave a trail of his own pheromones to confuse competitors. Thousands of female fireflies living along mangroves in Malaysia will simultaneously start flashing pulses of light up to 90 times a minute. Like the uniqueness of birdsongs, the rhythm of these flashes is species-specific, geared to attract the correct male. A few predators, however, can mimic these pulses and easily capture a love-struck male for dinner.

Most species seem to have relatively painless births (as best as we can tell) and multiple offspring. The elephant will have five to ten offspring in a lifetime, frogs produce thousands of eggs, fish tens of thousands of eggs, oysters hundreds of millions of eggs, and many lower plants trillions of spores. Some microorganisms can replicate themselves by the billions daily. Survival of the fittest can sometimes lie in numbers.

Many male species court females in ways that they were never taught. They certainly didn't see their parents' courtship dance. The male satin bowerbird builds a nest called a bower, which he paints blue using his beak and berry juices. To further entice the female with his wealth, he may add all kinds of blue trinkets he has scavenged from the neighborhood.

Another form of gifting is puddling. Male swordtail fish will pass ("puddle") nutrients with their sperm to the female during copulation. This will aid development of the young. Burrowing owls place gifts at the entrance to their homes, such as insect parts, cigarette butts, and tidbits of garbage. The male mannikin bird does a "moon dance" strut to attract females. Scorpions do a promenade, pulling their female partner over a packet of sperm that she sucks into her genital pore. Bank swallows pass a white feather back and forth. Albatrosses have a variety of very fancy dances that they use to arouse and interest each other.

We do a lot of the same things with flashy cars, eye-catching jewelry, bumper stickers, fashionable or alluring clothes, loud stereos, fragrant colognes, fat wallets, seductive dancing, white teeth, well-groomed physiques, and the right words said in the right way at the right time.

MATING

Male lions will mate for days, at an average of up to 300 encounters (somebody else counted this). Presumably the excess is needed for stimulating ovulation. An Australian marsupial mouse outdoes the lion; it copulates until it falls out of the tree exhausted and dies. Mating can last 12 hours, and the male may take on numerous partners before he's done for. One would think that the theory of evolution would favor the male not falling out of the tree.

After sniffing the female's urine to be sure it's time, the male gazelle goes through a ritual dance to persuade the female to copulate. In a like manner, the male elephant uses his trunk to check a female's urine. A collection of specialized tissues called the vomeronasal organ in the roof of his mouth (which we also have in our noses) tells him if she is in heat. Her hormones will cause the bull elephant to get an instant erection, and the process starts. How it all works is not clear, but her hormones may cause the production of nitric oxide which, in turn, makes the blood vessels in the penis dilate. It's similar to the way the medication Viagra works.

Some fish can change sex on demand. Female basslets can change color and grow male sex organs if the more brightly colored males die or are killed off. If a female clown fish dies, the male can activate his dormant ovaries, turn off his male sex organs, and fully function as a female. Several species of deep sea fish and mollusks are both sexes. They will release sperm and then eggs. This helps maintain the species if a mate is hard to find.

Dragonflies copulate on the wing. White-throated swifts copulate in midair with the so-called cloacal kiss. Dolphins and whales mate on the fin, as it were, rather quickly and from the front. A certain parasitic fly can lay its eggs inside an airborne bee. And there's a moth that hitchhikes on sloths. Every time the sloth has a bowel movement, it lays some eggs in it.

Songbirds may seem monogamous, but tests indicate that as many as a quarter of their eggs are fathered by other males. The male roadrunner, being not so attractive, brings his female a nuptial gift in his beak such as a scorpion or a field mouse. He approaches from her rear, wags his tail, and jumps up and down, trying to impress her. If there's something about his wagging or jumping she doesn't like, she leaves.

CHILD CARE

The female scorpion will eat the male after fertilization unless he stings her first to sedate her. Likewise, the black widow spider and the praying mantis enjoy eating their sperm donor. In contrast, window lace-weaver spiderlings will eat their mother, and garden spiderlings will often eat some of their brothers and sisters. Barbaric or not, it comes naturally and may have some maternal nutritional value. Fortunately that didn't evolve, or we would each be eating all of our neighbors.

There are numerous examples of improbable coincidences in childbirth and child-rearing patterns. The newborn giraffe is one. The baby giraffe is born with very sharp hooves, yet all extremities arrive encased in a gelatinous covering that protects the mother's birth canal from being torn apart. The covering falls off in a few days. Imagine how long this species would have lasted if each birth lead to a life-threatening laceration of the birth canal.

The pangolin is a scale-covered anteater in Uganda and Senegal; it defends itself by rolling into a ball covered with fish-scale-size, razor-sharp scales. Oddly, this species is born with soft scales that harden after two days. Again designed for survival? Could any of its ancestors have been born with a mantle of razors?

▓▓ PANGOLIN ▓▓

As is the case with many animals that have exterior armor that could damage their mother's birth canal and kill their parent, this Asian mammal's razorlike scales are soft at birth and harden soon after. Any intermediate form of hardened scales before delivery would have terminated the species.

© *Nigel J. Dennis / Photo Researchers, Inc.*[10]

Siamese fighting fish have a unique style of child-rearing. First, the male blows saliva-coated bubbles into a froth. After mating with the female, he puts each fertilized egg inside his mouth and carries them to the froth where he spits each individual one into its own bubble. He hangs around until the babies become free swimmers, catching any that may fall out prematurely and spitting them back into another, more intact bubble. This is very hard to explain using Darwin's ideas.

Many tropical frogs also build frothy nests where they lay several thousand eggs. The froth not only protects them from sunlight, but it has chemicals that deter predators and trap oxygen. When the off-spring have matured, they break out and drop to the water as tadpoles, ready to do what all frogs do without a hint of parental instruction.

The Amazon splash tetra lays its eggs on vertical leaves just above the water's surface. The female and male jump in perfect unison, land on the leaf together, simultaneously release eggs and sperm, and tumble back together into the water. They do this repeatedly in a synchronized way until all of the eggs are laid. Afterward, the father hangs around to keep the eggs moist by splashing them with his tail.

The cichlids of South America take protection to another level. The mother puts the eggs in her mouth as soon as they are fertil-ized and keeps them there until they are large enough to make it on their own or too large for her mouth. If they are not mature yet, some species will transfer them to the father's mouth. The gastric frog of Australia stops acid production to raise her tadpoles in her stomach. There cannot be a transitional form, or else the eggs would be digested. A Surinam toad raises its young under a translucent membrane on her back.

The kangaroo mother has two kinds of milk, one for the newborn and another, with less fat, for her juvenile. She can actually care for an embryo, a baby, and a juvenile at the same time.

Baby spiders, or hatchlings, do not seem to receive any instruc-tion on how to go about their life. They immediately know what to eat, where to go, and how to get there. Some disperse by ballooning, which they do by balancing themselves on their front two legs, then shooting off a sheet of silk that catches the wind and carries them far away. On occasion thousands can be seen aloft.

Like many other insects, spiders shed their outer body armor or molt to make room for the newer, larger version of themselves. They accomplish this task by expanding their body by taking in excess fluid. When the exoskeleton splits open, they climb out and then hang around until the newest body covering hardens in place. This process can take several minutes or all day, during which their unprotected or naked body is vulnerable to predation. The newest self will inflate its body further to allow for growing room in the new casing. This process occurs many times during their life cycle, and if they lose a leg, they can usually grow it back.

In an unusual reversal of fortune, the male sea horse becomes pregnant. The male grows a pouch and the female puts her eggs inside it to be fertilized. The pouch changes into a placenta-like pocket exuding a nutritious liquid. This seems to be a flip-flop that requires all systems working simultaneously.

The monarch butterfly doesn't actually raise its young, but it gives them the needed tools. They change to adults, like many insects and a few amphibians, by a process called metamorphosis. The eggs are purposefully laid on the underneath side of the leaves of a milkweed plant. When they change to caterpillars, they eat the egg casing and then the milkweed leaf. The leaves give them potential predator poison for storage. It is harmless to them. During the first two weeks the caterpillar increases its weight 3000-fold. Soon thereafter, it becomes a packet-like pupa hanging from the bottom of a leaf. Here it metamorphoses into a beautiful butterfly. Its beauty is partly a warning to predators that says, "Eat me and you'll die." Could there have been intermediate butterflies who tasted this leaf and died off? Not likely.

■ ■ ■ ■ ■

The procreation and perpetuation of a new generation is an intricate endeavor that allows very little room for error. Most offspring do not have the advantages of learning life skills at home over several years, or renting a how-to video. Instead, they have to make their way guided by a complex internal book of instructions. Should a few pages be missing or the words be blurred, the species might perish.

26. OTHER UNUSUAL INSTINCTS

"Our Heavenly Father invented man because He was disappointed in the monkey."

—MARK TWAIN

Can animals instinctively sense natural disasters? Some people think so. There are stories about rats fleeing cities just before earthquakes hit. Dogs will act crazy and horses will jump fences that normally contain them. Twelve hours before Hurricane Charley struck Florida in 2004, 14 electronically tagged sharks off Sarasota fled into deep water. They apparently had never left that area before. They stayed away for two weeks. Although thousands of people perished in Sri Lanka during the December 2004 tsunami, reportedly, none of the elephants, deer, or other wild animals died. They all fled in advance of the calamity. Could it be they have an additional instinct that we lack? Or are these stories unsubstantiated? Some theories propose that certain volatile chemicals or faint vibrations precede some events, like earthquakes, which only animals can detect and somehow know to flee.

SYNCHRONY

Synchronization is an inherently natural and seemingly instinctual phenomenon. It is defined as a coincidence in time, meaning things happen together either by accident or by design, such as the simultaneous lip movement and audible words of a movie character

How Do They Know?

The blister beetle larva knows how to catch a ride with a male bee. It emits a scent which is identical to a female bee. When the male bee arrives to mate, as many as 2000 larvae will climb on board and hitch a ride until he finds a real female. That's where they disembark and feast on the pollen. There are flower mites that run up the beaks of hummingbirds, hitch a ride inside their nostrils, and disembark at the next flower. An Australian desert frog buries itself about a foot underground when the land dries up. To survive it forms a skintight body suit to retain moisture until the rains return. It has two nostril tubes that connect to the surface for air.

The red-and-green macaws of Peru can eat poisonous fruits after they ingest riverbank clays that detoxify these poisons. The maroon leaf monkey of Borneo aids its digestion by eating clay from termite mounds beforehand. If this clay is not taken from a specific part of the termite nest, a banana might kill him.

or paired ice skaters at the Olympics. Simultaneous timing can be found in the earth's rotation with the seasons, lunar phases with tides, and light waves in laser beams. Flip on a light switch and every electron along the wire seems to get excited at the same moment.

Reading this book is a function of synchronizing your anatomy and physiology. We think by synchronizing the actions of trillions of brain cells. We move by synchronizing billions of muscle cells, bone cells, and ligament cells. We feel pain by synchronizing and processing the sensations in nerve endings. Our bladders collect urine in a synchronized way and our gastrointestinal tract digests food in a synchronized manner.

If one places a single heart cell in a petri dish, it will beat at a specific rate. Then, add a few more heart cells to the same petri dish. At first some may beat at different rates, but they soon find one another and coordinate the beating. This is the kind of synchronicity that keeps us alive. Billions of heart cells situated in the SA node of our heart simultaneously send off an electrical impulse that travels through the heart at 60 to 100 times a minute. Each impulse causes the organ to pump blood. If this node were damaged, perhaps by trauma or a heart attack, another group of pacemaker cells would take over, also firing in a repeating manner to keep us alive. Scientists call the mechanism an internal resettable oscillator, and the body has a number of backup functions built in.

Fireflies have a similar phenomenon. At mating time, hundreds of thousands of these insects will simultaneously light up and pulse their lights in unison. It's not one light starting and then two, followed by ten or one hundred. They all simultaneously begin together on some unclear signal. Place a firefly in a dark room and it will pulse at a natural rate. Place several more in the same room and they will soon coordinate with each other. Crickets and croaking frogs also synchronize.

A flock of birds will turn one direction or another, swoop down, take off, land, and bank at the same moment. Fast-speed filming has shown that this is not a follow-the-leader phenomenon but a simultaneous group decision. Likewise, a school of fish will also swim in perfect synchrony, acting more like one large fish than dozens of separate members. Grunions will come ashore for synchronous breeding during the first, highest tide in spring every year. No evolutionist has clearly shown why.

There is the mass spawning on coral reefs, wherein all of the coral beings release their eggs and sperm at precisely the same moment. Lunar phase and water temperature are thought to be triggering events. A feeding frenzy follows, but the massive numbers of offspring virtually guarantees random fertilizations and perpetuation of the species.

For unclear reasons, millions of locusts simultaneously irrupt from hibernation every 17 years and immediately begin a month of mating and ravaging the countryside. The 1874 swarm in the Midwest was described as 300 miles wide and over a half mile deep. Their combined weight was in excess of 25 million tons, and they ate more than 80,000 tons of crops.

Every year at precisely the same time the Pacific palolo worm reverses itself inside its tubular home and grows reproductive organs at the exposed end, which break off and swim to the surface as if they were separate organisms. They even have primitive eyes. En route to the surface each becomes a bag of sperm or eggs. At a given moment millions of these bags break open. The West Indian counterpart does exactly the same thing at a different but precise moment. How many successful intermediates were needed on this one?

Microorganisms can also act in synchrony. A prime example is a pathogenic virus or bacteria in our intestines. One would think the presence of one or two of these individuals would be insignificant or have only the barest impact. Instead, many species enclose themselves in a polymeric matrix called a *biofilm*. This protects them from antibiotics, toxins, immune cells, and antibodies until they reach a high enough density (population). At a predetermined certain head count or critical mass, also called *quorum sensing,* they simultaneously release deadly toxins. That's why someone can go from feeling well to being at death's door within hours.

Science does not have a good explanation of how biological synchronicity came about.

PART SIX
IMPROBABLE NATURAL COMMUNICATIONS

> "Half the world is composed of people
> who have something to say and
> can't, and the other half who have
> nothing to say and keep on saying it."
>
> — ROBERT FROST

Communication is the interaction between two or more living beings that begins with the desire to send information and usually ends with reception of the information. It is much more than just talking, squawking, or chirping. It requires numerous macro-, micro-, and submicro-anatomical capabilities to send the correct signals to other individuals who must have the comparable macro-, micro-, and submicro-neurological capabilities to receive them, process the information, and then the ability to return meaningful responses. Even the lack of an answer can be meaningful. How bad is the message if you walk into a crowded, noisy room and everyone abruptly stops talking? Or if you're sitting around a campfire and the forest suddenly goes silent?

At dusk and dawn, nearly everywhere short of the North Pole and the peaks of mountains like Mt. Everest, one can hear a barrage of sound from insects, birds, reptiles, and a few mammals extolling their virtues and discussing sex. Schooling fish release a chemical communication when under attack. Trees release chemicals to alert others of a different kind of danger. We all talk. According to researchers at UCLA, even yeast cells communicate by vibrating at 1000 times per second.

Communication is vital to survival, and it can involve a single sense or any combination. It might even be that ill-defined sixth sense—"I smell trouble"; "I can feel what they're thinking." A fist held high tells you a lot, as does a simple smile or a baby's cry.

Some kind of communication seems to exist in all living beings. There is an incredible array of mechanisms, frequencies, amplitudes, dialects, styles, "words," songs, and alarms used. Many species send messages that are outside our abilities to detect: sounds, colors, markings, UV light, infrared heat, and aromas. The use of body language is universal and uniquely understood. It can incorporate dancing, stomping, flashing lights, playing, electrical shocks, spitting, hissing, echolocating, rattling, yawning, sneezing, coughing, vibrating, body-color changes, throwing things, strutting, pouting, defecating, urinating, fornicating, salivating, weaving, rapping, caressing, bowing, vomiting, buzzing, flapping, body-shape changes, spraying, body-size changes, marking territories, begging, charging, coiling, feigning an injury or death, kissing, hugging, crying, posturing, or touching. A single wink can send a clear message.

Man may be the only animal who deals in abstract communications. Maybe he's the only animal who cares to. No evolutionist, to date, has ever adequately explained why humans have gone on to complex cerebral concerns that have nothing to do with the instincts of survival. Poetry is a good example. So are reminiscing, multiplying 1012 by 312, playing the flute, competing in sports, and designing video games.

Although we rarely notice, three-quarters of our communication is nonverbal. Note the everyday handshake and whether it was limp or strong or if it was even offered. We accentuate and modify nearly everything we say with some type of body motion, sometimes even when we're on the telephone. What does a person mean when they connect a roll of their eyes upward with a comment? Or what if the same exact remark is followed by a deep sigh? Or a laugh? A single fist held high could mean defiance; one hand held open and one closed could be a child's game; tight fists held close-to-body could mean imminent danger; fists held high could mean victory; and hands pressed together, prayer. Look at sign language. There are approximately 750,000 meaningful hand gestures.

■■■■■

Many species send deceptive messages. Certain caterpillars resemble bird excrement to discourage predation, some flies look like bees to scare off would-be predators, a walking stick looks like an unpalatable real stick. A few animals and certain plants have a hellacious odor or an obnoxious taste to attract or discourage insects and some animals, like the hognose snake, pretend to be dead. An opossum collapses into a motionless, deathlike state and exudes a putrid secretion from its anal glands. The forked-tongue beetle will feign death, withdrawing its legs into special grooves and everting foul-smelling glands at its rear end. It seems very clear that these all-or-nothing maneuvers were designed for survival. I can't see any use for them in partial or transitional measures.

Some scientists think humans are the only animals who truly feel and share emotions, but there are many people who say they are wrong. Some of us like to think we are the only animals that can interact in emotional ways, but again there is a lot of anecdotal evidence suggesting many animals feel fear, caution, excitement, pleasure, love, grief, and sorrow. Meerkats appear to console a dying relative; penguins bellow when their young die; a bear will help an injured sibling catch fish; and elephants shed tears at their clan's burial sites. My cat spits at me when I try to put him to bed. My dog wags his tail when I come home. Of course, he wags his tail when I leave in the morning too. Just ask any pet owner if their cat or dog feels emotion. The answer will be a definitive yes.

The Expression of Emotions in Man and Animals by Darwin might have been the first significant book to argue for animal communications and a better piece of work than *The Origins of Species.* In it, he wrote,

> Nevertheless the difference in mind between man and
> the higher animals, great as it is, certainly is one of degree

and not of kind. We have seen that the senses and intuitions, the various emotions and faculties, such as love, memory, attention, curiosity, imitation, reason, etc., of which man boasts may be found in an incipient, or even sometimes in a well-developed condition, in the lower animals.

The question arises, however, could the ability to convey one's feelings or thoughts have come about by random accidents of evolution or survival of the fittest? Did humans learn how to verbalize one word, then eons later utter a phrase or two, and then after another string of eons speak a sentence? Or did the whole communication capability (speech part of brain, nerves, tongue, mouth, lips, ears, and the hearing part of brain) explode on the scene? Just moving the tongue is more complicated than safely driving a car with 12 steering wheels and dozens of gas pedals, brakes, and turn signals. Then add in the movement of lips, mouth, vocal cords, and lungs to get out one word. And don't forget the neurological pathways to change the volume, tone, and inflections at will. Billions of nerve cells are involved. Having the knowledge (and desire) to warn someone of impending danger evolve without a mechanical way to shout it to another species member, who may or may not have the ability to hear it, makes no sense at all. It seems like a complex machine showed up in its entirety just when we needed it.

For obvious reasons we don't know a thing about prehistoric communications. The grumbling or roaring sounds we associate with T. rex are mere movie creations. Perhaps those animals were mute or made sounds like King Kong. Many professionals have thought that dinosaurs were the ancestor to birds, but there are increasing doubts. Recent findings in northeastern China clearly show pterosaurs (a reptile) had feathers, but they also had teeth, and their wings were a function of their hands, not their arms. The paleontology evidence is also mounting, if evolution is correct, that these reptiles might have had the same remote ancestors as birds. If so, did they caw, twitter, or sing?

So far, however, that ancestor remains unnamed and unfound.

Whichever way communication came about, logic would dictate that the anatomy had to be there first. Certainly, the brain didn't have the ability to talk with "nowhere to go." *Hey, I really have something to say, but no mouth or hands to tell you.* Or, *I have these vocal cords but no use for them.* One might guess it all began with simple, primitive sounds, but the mechanical changes needed to get to our present level are huge. These are not a few mutations or a function of survival of the fittest. According to Dr. Ian Tattersall, humans had a vocal tract that could produce the sounds of articulate speech over a half million years before we have evidence our forbears used language. How could that happen? Was it preprogrammed? Did some primate group have the ability to talk, but no language skills, by accident? Also, no one seems to have a clue where (or how) echolocation or bioluminescence arose.

Not only did our predecessors make meaningful sounds, but the sounds they made were in the right range for others of their own kind to hear. Imagine the impact on survival if early humans couldn't hear what they were saying because their ears were tuned to a different frequency. Or what if they didn't have ears? Or a mother couldn't hear her infant crying? Perhaps, one might say, survival of the fittest weeded out all primates who were tuned to the wrong frequency, but that's very doubtful.

The idea that speech, vision, and hearing evolved in step along with extensive brain matter is like imagining you can build a city by simultaneously bringing in a number of modular Sears Towers—the Eye Tower, the Ear Tower, and the Mega-Brain Tower. These are not simple processes or simple structures. If these senses came about by evolution, it would have required the gradual and purposeful changing (and adding on) of billions of neurological, musculo-skeletal, and sensory connections that interact (correctly!) on a millisecond-by-millisecond basis.

27. CHEMICAL AND VISUAL SIGNALS

"I'd love to think of nature as an unlimited broadcasting station, through which God speaks to us every hour, if we will only tune in."

—GEORGE WASHINGTON CARVER

All living beings send and receive chemical (invisible) signals. Many can have a major impact on day-to-day activity, such as mating and social behavior. Easily recognized chemical signals are the smell of newly baked bread or someone's cologne. What you actually sense is millions of chemical compounds bombarding thousands of very sophisticated olfactory cells in your nose, which change these structural items to electrical signals for your brain to process. This sense also tells you whether something is edible, spoiled, or decaying. There are countless, sometimes lifesaving, examples of important messages that depend on invisible olfactory messages.

■■■■■

One chemical signal that has received a lot of press is the sex hormone or pheromone, which is a word taken from the Greek for "transfer" and "excitement." It creates and accelerates sexual attraction, especially at estrus time. In humans, pheromones waft from specialized skin glands in armpits, beards, and pubic areas and are picked up by the vomeronasal organ, a small clump of specialized tissue located along the nasal septum. At one time this organ was thought to be vestigial, perhaps the holes left over from reptiles like the pit viper, but the data is steadily increasing that the cellular receptors in those holes have a major impact on our behavior.

Like thyroid hormones traversing the bloodstream, pheromones transfer their messages across open space. They can cause a bull to smash down a fence or elephants to fight for a female in heat. An unspayed cat will spray pheromones to let would-be suitors know it's available. Most of the animal world depends on these signals to tell them when it's time to reproduce; all other times, most animals remain relatively uninterested in sexual intercourse. Perhaps this was designed to avoid wasting calories at non-estrus moments. Looking at the theory of evolution, one would have to ask how a different system could have worked. If animals did not know when it was time, they might die of fatigue and malnourishment.

College women living in the same dormitory will have their menstrual cycles automatically synchronized (called McClintock effect) by invisible chemical signals. The thought, presumably, is that having all females ready to conceive at the same time aids time management by the males, who need to be out hunting for food. Another type of signal accompanies vomiting. This message makes others feel like vomiting, too, and seems to say, *I've eaten something that might be bad for you too.* Perfumes (a signal) attract, and body odor (another meaningful signal) detracts. There is a cultural component to this, however. Napoléon instructed Josephine to keep an apple in her armpit for him to enjoy later on.

A female mouse can tell, by pheromones, whether a male is healthy or infected with parasites. Her vomeronasal organ senses will not allow her to pick an ill partner. Male elephants will check a female's urine via the vomeronasal organ to see if she's receptive. Where are the missing links on this one? Generally, female animals prefer the smell of the most dominant male, perhaps because his offspring will be the strongest; whereas males will respond to any female pheromone. In some species males will even attempt to have sex with a male who has just had sex with a female. The scientific guess is that the female hormone has rubbed off or because there's no one else to practice on, but no one knows.

Pheromones are extremely common signals among insects. These are divided into nine major groups: sex, aggregation, dispersal, alarm, trail following, territorial, job description, funeral, and invitation. Termites have several types of glands along the abdominal cavity for marking territory, queen bees use pheromones to attract drones, the Douglas fir female beetle releases pheromones to attract males once she completes her burrow, and sentry fire ants emit an alarm pheromone whenever an intruder enters their residence. The large number of glands per insect and numerous chemical signals found among insects indicates this is a very complex interaction that would have had extreme difficulty evolving by accident. One might ask, what was the attractant in the pre-pheromone days?

The Match Game

Mammals often carry the scent of social dominance or submission; the stronger the scent, the more powerful the individual. Elephants exude a liquid from beneath their eyes that changes from a honey scent to something awful resembling old goats, yet very pleasing to female elephants. The worse it smells, the more powerful the animal. Mothers can identify their newborn offspring by their scent as if they were wearing name tags. There is evidence to suggest these wafting hormones, just like a birdsong and healthy plumage, tell individual animals who's a good genetic match and who isn't.

VISUAL SIGNALS

Bright colors such as yellow, red, blue, and orange tell or remind predators that this species is not tasty, at a minimum, and is likely poisonous. They are like giant STOP signs. If an animal gets sick eating a yellow toad, so the thinking goes, that animal will never eat another yellow toad. He or she might even pass this function on to friends and neighbors. There is a chance that some species innately know to avoid certain colors.

There are three species of poisonous frogs that are marked with very bright colors. One of the most venomous is the poison-dart frog found in Central and South America. The local Indians would roast them over a fire to extract the poison that exudes from their pores. An animal needs to merely lick this frog and it's all over. Strangely, the same frog raised in a pet store will not be poisonous (that's a good thing). Instead, it makes this poison after eating certain insects in its home environment. How this phenomenon evolved in prehistoric times is yet to be adequately explained.

Plants also send messages with colors. An unripe berry or fruit will remain green until it's ready to be eaten. They turn brown from rot when it's not safe. Plants also add or change scents to sort out these decisions. Some change consistency or texture as well.

Poisonous snakes may not always be brightly marked, but other visuals include telltale fangs and a triangular head. The extremely deadly copperhead has very bright warning bands of red, black, and yellow. The pit viper has a visible pit between its eyes that it uses to sense infrared—warm-blooded prey. Rattlesnakes may shake their head first (another visual clue) and then shake their rattlers before striking.

There are venomous insects and arachnids hiding everywhere. Fortunately, some have very distinctive visual warnings. The brown recluse spider has a brown violin shaped image on the back of its body and the black widow usually has a red, white, or orange hour-glass on its abdomen. The scorpion has an obvious tail with a stinger. The wasp is easily identified.

Butterflies may have giant eyes on their wings to scare predators. The monarch butterfly is brightly colored and thereby marked as poisonous. There are mimics, like the viceroy butterfly, a near twin, who benefit from a similar look. The larva of the lobster moth looks like a scorpion. Amphibians, like newts and salamanders, are notoriously toxic and often will have bright colors to advertise their danger.

Many species use simultaneous sound and visual signals for communication during courtship. The black sicklebill, a bird of paradise in New Guinea, sings out at dawn when it's still quiet. As the female approaches, he puffs out in brilliant colors of aqua and violet. The blue bird of paradise, who is among the most beautiful birds in the world, first attracts his mate with a dance done hanging upside down from a branch. He displays changing blue and violet colors by flexing his feathers and expands and contracts an oval patch on his chest. He concludes with a buzzing mating call.

■ ■ ■ ■ ■

Could there have been transitional, relatively useless signals preceding these very meaningful and complex messages as different species moved up the tree of evolution? Very unlikely. Signals had to work. By definition, a signal without meaning is not a signal. It's a noise.

28. IN THE REALMS OF THE BIOSPHERE

> "This we know: The earth does not belong to man, man belongs to the Earth. All things are connected like the blood that unites us all. Man did not weave the web of life, he is merely a strand in it. Whatever he does to the web, he does to himself."
>
> —ATTRIBUTED TO CHIEF SEATTLE

Communication is designed to find food, sound alarms, express pleasure, attract sexual partners, discourage competitors, mimic, confuse, chase off predators, make friends, warn enemies, entertain, console, instruct the young, threaten, recruit help, identify foe or friend, surrender, submit, call for help, and express emotions. Naturalist Eugene Morton breaks down animal sounds into eight different meanings by their harshness within the categories of barks, growls, and whines.

Every species seems to have one or more unique ways to send messages. Like AM and FM radio stations, certain frequencies are owned; sometimes several are used, to perhaps better cover their bases. These messages convey important information that may have been purposefully encrypted for privacy and protection. Other than the obvious growls, barks, or hisses that blatantly say, "Get out of here!" even those species who are closest on the evolutionary scale don't seem to understand each other. Most likely, they never have and never will. And why would they? Why would rabbits communicate in ways their predators could understand? Or bears comprehend the dance of bees? Imagine a hunted fox shouting to his comrades in hound-dog talk where he was about to hide.

ON THE LAND

A very good example of animal communication can be found among vervets—Old World monkeys who live south of the Sahara. In studies published by Seyfarth and Cheney in 1977 and 1978, these monkeys were found to have specific alarm calls for leopard, eagle, and snake. Given a specific alarm signal their extended family would quickly head to the ground or up the trees for safety. Misunderstanding these "words" and going the wrong direction could be a fatal mistake. Also, mother vervets, like many other species around the world, were seen to recognize distress calls from their own infants. Tape recordings of this same distress call would evoke identical responses.

Another intriguing example comes from research by Dr. Constantine N. Slobodchikoff of Northern Arizona University, done on prairie dogs. His findings suggest this rodent has unique alarm calls for different predators and descriptive "words" in its vocalizations too. Dr. Slobodchikoff made recordings of alarm calls over three days while humans of all types and sizes walked past the prairie dogs' colonies. Some participants wore white lab coats; others wore brightly colored T-shirts. The results showed that these animals had a specific alarm call for humans but encoded additional information into their vocalizations that may have related the color of their clothes, general shape of the intruders, or their degree of concern.

Certain monkeys, octopi, and dolphins will pass on newly learned useful skills to their counterparts. Chimpanzees are often cited as having the capability to communicate using sign language and lexigrams (printed symbols). Because of an evolutionary riddle, primates cannot talk as we do, but they can understand the meaning of many words. They can also put some together. In the 1980s, a bonobo chimp named Kanzi learned to construct 650 sentences at the Georgia State University Language Research Center. It happened while researchers were trying to teach his adopted mother, Matata. He was an uninterested infant at the time. His mother never did learn the symbols, but he ultimately surprised the researchers by piecing together such sentences as "Go scare Matata with the snake," "Pour Coke in the lemonade," and "Give doggie some yogurt." These would not be terribly helpful in the wild, but they were extremely insightful.

It has long been thought that giraffes were mute, but recent studies have found they communicate through infrasonic or subsonic sounds. These are communications we cannot hear. They swing their necks up and back to make this low-frequency sound, but there's much to be learned yet.

The Elephant

Elephants communicate over hundreds of miles by subsonic messages as well. During estrus, the female elephant will emit a series of these communications, which are actually a song, telling nearby bulls

---

Setting Borders

Territorial signals are common and are reminiscent of our posted signs *Trespassers Will Be Shot* or *Beware of Dog*. Capturing a manageable chunk of territory and holding it are extremely important for protecting one's home and family, having enough space to find food, knowing the lay of the land, and attracting future mates. Spiders set out ambushes to protect their homes; plants even fight over sunny spots.

Many mammals, including canines, will mark their property with urine. Certain monkeys leave a brown, oily fluid, a secretion from an anal gland on the edge of their boundaries. How could that have possibly evolved? One would think they'd have to had gotten it right the first time.

---

that it is time for mating. They take advantage of sound channels in the atmosphere much like the finback whales do in the deep ocean. These are invisible channels of cool air trapped by upper warm layers. They occur in the late afternoon and keep the sound waves contained for hundreds of miles. The siren song will typically travel for as far as 60 square miles. She uses her trunk with its 60,000 muscles like a musical instrument, changing notes and frequencies like a trumpet player with dozens of piston valves.

Much of the work on elephant communication was done by Joyce Poole and Cynthia Moss at the Amboseli Elephant Research Project in Kenya. They have discovered the meaning of 30 different elephant calls. About 70 percent of them are not audible to the human ear. Their greeting rumble compares with our excited hug. Another is a repeating contact call that makes sure members of the herd are still within ear range. The musth rumble is a male's response to the estrus call, excitedly telling her he's ready. And then there's family pandemonium, with screams of excitement, defecation, urination, and temporal gland secretions when the female bride returns to the group. Fortunately, evolution dropped that response and replaced it with making toasts and throwing rice.

Elephant feet are extremely sensitive to vibrations. They seem to sense, by standing on their toenails, approaching thunderstorms and will head in that direction in hopes of finding water. There are numerous reports that they can sense earthquakes and tsunamis—and indeed, elephants in Phuket, Thailand, began wailing minutes before the December 2004 tsunami struck, broke their chains, and fled uphill. Hippos were reported to have bolted from a Malaysian zoo at the same pre-crisis moment. This type of sensing is being studied for possible early warning systems in the future.

Elephants also use body language commonly, and there are very distinct meanings associated with the flapping of their ears, trumpeting, and shaking of their trunks. It is readily apparent they can recognize each other and know how to work together. A very distinct, seemingly sad, response can be seen whenever the subsonic sounds of a deceased member of the group are replayed on tape.

■ ■ ■ ■ ■

Mice sing to each other too. They primarily use ultrasonic squeaks to pass on information about two octaves above human hearing, but occasionally a squeak can actually be heard by children, who have the best hearing. The mice actually stand on their hind legs and can be seen with their mouths open, their throats inflated, and their bodies vibrating. Timothy E. Holy and Zhongsheng Guo at Washington University in St. Louis say the complexity of their songs are comparable to bird and whale songs.

Snakes communicate. The North American bull snake emits a bellowing cow-like grunt that can easily be heard far away. The Bornean cave racer snake emits a meow type of sound. No one knows how this odd sound came about, but professionals speculate that it might be used to attract small birds or interfere with bat echolocation. The king cobra has special pockets off its trachea to make growling hisses. Grass snakes have been reported to make birdlike calls and pythons make a deer-like bleat. One can easily presume these sounds have a definite purpose. Each sound requires the proper anatomy, physiology, coordination of brain function, and complex vocalizing apparatuses.

IN THE SEA

Underwater species seem to communicate for the same reasons land species do. They make use of sounds, chemicals, lights, electrical shocks, body colors, and body language. Some fish actually hum. After migrating from the deep Pacific to the U.S. coastline, midshipman fish will hum a love song, which is described as a motorboat drone. They do this to attract females. They can also make grunts and growls when guarding their nests. The weakfish makes a purring sound and the drum fish makes a drumming sound. Over 208 species off the North American coasts have been shown to make meaningful, species-specific sounds, including catfish, groupers, eels, and crabs. Several varieties of shrimp are known for making a lot of racket.

Whales and Dophins

Many water species make sounds that we can't hear. This field of study has been steadily expanding for years. Dolphins converse in frequencies above our hearing range and whales communicate far below our capabilities. Hippos, a part-time water species, also have a subsonic language.

The calls of the blue whale and finback can be detected for

thousands of miles. The blue whale is the loudest; it is able to reach 190 decibels, which is louder than the loudest crowd at a college football game. Whales utilize the sound fixing and ranging (SOFAR) channel, found at a depth of 3000 feet. This is a submarine layer of water created by differences in temperature, pressure, and salinity. It confines their calls to a narrow band that can reach from one continent to another. The anatomy, the songs, and the natural channel are unique coincidences.

Humpback whales are often called the grand musicians of the sea and their songs are frequently described as haunting. Testing a new technology, the U.S. Navy secretly recorded many of these songs during the 1950s with the Sound Surveillance System (SOSUS). In 1970, Roger Payne used an underwater microphone to record an album called *Songs of the Humpback Whale*. One question that arises is, did whale songs become louder in the past as the continents separated? If so, how? The scientific evidence is loudly absent.

It turns out, humpback songs have as many as nine themes, lasting up to 15 minutes. They can vary from year to year. Because most singing takes place during breeding season, scientists have assumed the purpose is to attract females and discourage competitors. The songs also give information about their strength, health, and size. It's sort of like our teenagers with their loud car stereos.

Dolphins might be the smartest animal on the planet, man included. They can be taught to use touchpads and keyboards, and some scientists think they will be the first species with whom we will eventually converse. Some professionals actually think they can be taught to speak as we do. They travel in herds as large as a thousand and each member seems to have a unique signature whistle or audible name. They are the only animals we know of who carry naturally given names. Naming happens shortly after birth and mothers will often use the "name" when trying to find a calf whenever they've been separated. Individual adults will also call out the name to find specific others in a crowd of dolphins or stay in touch with an individual who is out of sight. Coincidental skill?

Dolphins converse with whistles, burst-pulse sounds, click trains, raspberries, groans, and a host of body movements, such as slapping their tail flukes against the water and bumping into each other. Whistles are high-frequency sounds that are out of our hearing range. Burst-pulse sounds are the usual barks, squeals, and squawks heard in films. Click trains are sonar clicks that cycle at about ten per second but can increase to 400 cycles as they approach another object. Their skills are so keen that they can distinguish a kernel of corn from a BB at 50 feet, distinguish different foils of metal, and pinpoint the location of underwater mines.

These clicks emanate from the melon, which is a large organ in their forehead. Scientists aren't sure where the sound waves come out. Dolphins receive the sonic echoes in their lower jaw, a hollow bone, and convert them to 3-D images on a microsecond-by-microsecond basis. This might be a virtual internal holographic theater. A sonar apparatus of this sophistication would have required millions of previous steps (links), yet there is no clear beginning in the fossil record.

■ ■ ■ ■ ■

According to Tim Friend, author of *Animal Talk*, electrical fields are used as communication tools by a variety of aquatic species, including sharks, eels, and some fish. They use them to sense prey and communicate with other members of their own species. Knife fish sing an electric duet when mating and can change the frequencies to protect themselves from eavesdropping eels. Under laboratory conditions an eel in a tank will blast and melt an underwater transmitter playing the knife fish song with 300 to 400 volts.

Bioluminescence or biological light is a common way of communication among species that live below 500 feet in the ocean. According to some deep sea reports, the dark seas can look like a dark night sky studded with twittering stars. Because these are areas that the sun cannot reach, a variety of species have adopted light signals for mating, attracting prey, and scaring off competitors. The ugly angler

An Alarming Phenomenon

It seems as if all species can communicate distress. One oddball that stands out is the screaming Budgett's frog. This Paraguay native is a two-hands-wide amphibian that resembles a cow patty. This unappetizing image normally protects it from predators, but should the patty camouflage fail, the frog inflates its body, rises up on its toes and, with mouth wide open, screams loudly like a person in distress.

fish uses a lighted lure that hangs in front of its huge jaws. Estimates to make this happen are in the range of 1000 different types of proteins. Some species use other biological species trapped within their bodies to do the lighting, such as a luminescent bacteria in pockets below the eyes or along the lateral flanks.

IN THE AIR

There are countless allusions to the beauty and inspiration of birdsongs in books, poetry, songs, and stories. We rejoice at hearing birds sing. Indeed, we probably should. They announce the beginning of a new day; they let us know it's the end of a hard season; and their songs are mostly happy melodies. Then again, what if you knew what the words were? Scientists think some of these are rather frank conversations about sex and are loaded with seductive comments, braggings about personal property, and vaunting sexual prowess. Who knows, they may be loaded with disguised expletives.

The sandhill crane, which migrates between the Canadian Arctic and Mexico, has the loudest bird call in the world. Its windpipe is longer than its height of four feet. This pipe winds around like a tuba beneath its breastbone. The call is a resonant *garoooo* that can carry for two miles. When thousands simultaneously make their calls, some observers have called the orchestration overwhelmingly eerie.

Bird calls include chirps, hoots, tweets, honks, peeps, squawks, screeches, screams, bill snaps, coos, whistles, clucks, churrs, chits, warbles, whining, yodels, squeals, carols, and trills. Scientists think every aspect of these utterances has meaning. Each sound is unique to each breed, and all aspects suggest Design. How would different breeds sort out who's singing or calling if they all whistled the same tune?

Singing requires billions of interacting brain cells, muscle cells, and sensory cells. The genetic template to sing these songs is present in all bird brains from the beginning, but newborns need to hear their parents sing early on if they are to lock in their breeding songs. Professionals in England have noticed a decline in songbirds, and although the reason may be pollution, it may also be too much noise. This causes birds to learn their songs incorrectly and severely impacts attracting mates later on.

We all come with specialized genetic templates to copy and learn from our parents. Or else our children might hiss like the family cat. Timing is also critical. If one patches a newborn cat's eye, it will, despite normal anatomy, remain blind in that eye forever. There seems to be a built-in opportune time to learn many of our skills.

Duets or duels are common between male and female birds. They are a means to attract one another and a way to maintain the relationship, protect one another, and keep track of each other's whereabouts. Many animals carry on less melodious duets, but gibbons are an exception. They are often cited as singing the most beautiful ones.

Birds communicate in ways other than songs. Albatrosses will hiss, clap their beaks together, and flap their wings when an intruder approaches. They also have a courtship dance that involves clapping their beaks together, head bobs, circling steps, head shaking, neck craning, moos, and whines. It seems as if this whole choreography was inherited.

The word's still out on how smart parrots might be. There are a few around who can identify textures and piece words together. Some ravens can mimic any sound in their environment, including a toilet flushing.

Insects

Insects communicate in ways we are only beginning to understand. The death's-head hawkmoth, with its skull-like marking and high-pitched squeaks that only children can hear, has been known for centuries. It will create a pulse sound at 280 pulses per minute, pause intermittently, and do it again. Scientists' best guess, since the moths suck honey from beehives without being attacked, is that their sound mimics sounds made by a queen bee. If so, any preliminary or transition sounds would have eliminated the species.

Tim Friend writes that the most complex system of communication next to that of humans is found in the dance steps of the honeybee. The round dance, or running in a circle, tells of nearby worthwhile sites. The transition dance, which resembles a half moon or sickle, addresses places that are an intermediate distance away. And the waggle dance, wherein the forager makes a figure eight with a "waggle" through the middle, gives information about the nectar or pollen location that may be more than 250 feet distant.

According to Dr. Karl P.N. Shuker, if the waggle dance is perpendicularly upward, fly directly into the sun; if perpendicularly downward, fly directly away from the sun; if the dancer moves upward and 30° to the left of perpendicular, fly into the sun and 30° left of it; and if the dancer moves downward and 30° to the right of perpendicular, fly away from the sun and 30° to the right of it. They must be smart—this is hard enough for people to follow. Simultaneous buzzing or vibrating adds further information. Every bee knows the language. Scientists, as yet, do not know if this is inherited or learned.

■ ■ ■ ■ ■

Communication skills require incredibly complex mechanisms on both the sending and the receiving end. Sometimes, even on the intercepting end. Modern investigations using much more sophisticated tools than those available during the 1800s and early 1900s have made Darwin's old, simplistic theories untenable and irrelevant.

PART SEVEN
IMPROBABLE
CONFESSIONS

29. IS DARWINISM DISGUISED RELIGION?

"If evolution is the explanation, then
evolution has a lot of explaining to do."

—THE PRESENT AUTHOR

Darwin believed that the acquisition of favorable, meaning the fittest, traits could be easily passed on to future generations and that this process would eventually result in newer, improved species. He borrowed this premise from Jean de Lamarck, an early 1800s biologist, who has long since been discredited by academia. Lamarck theorized that any favorable skill could be transferred via "gemmules" to a specie's reproductive organs and then to the offspring. With the exception of some esoteric antibody transfers, and extremely current epigenetic findings, however, there is no evidence a gemmule has ever existed.

This is not about the fastest cheetah giving birth to a faster breed of cheetahs or a darker moth surviving the polluted industrial days of nineteenth-century England. Those kinds of improved adaptations are already programmed into their genes. All species seem to have "just-in-case" programs or options in place, just like chameleons who change color. We form calluses on our hands to lessen injury with manual labor only if we need them, cease having menstrual periods during wars and famines to lessen births and thereby lessen starvation, vomit food when it seems spoiled, run fevers when infected to kill the intruding bacteria, and produce more red blood cells when climbing mountains, where oxygen tensions are lower.

▄▄ LAMARCK'S THEORY ▄▄

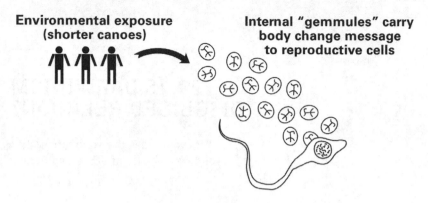

Environmental exposure (shorter canoes)

Internal "gemmules" carry body change message to reproductive cells

Result: A new generation of South American Indians with shorter legs for shorter canoes

Darwin borrowed heavily from Lamarck's theory of *use and disuse,* which has long since been discredited by modern science. The idea of "use it or lose it" is not true in reproduction. For example, Darwin speculated that a shortage of wood in South America could lead to shorter canoes with less legroom—and this would ultimately cause natives to be born with shorter legs.

Illustration by Dana Csakany.

This is more about a lizard whose tail was accidentally cut off and then, somehow, realizing that without a tail it was able to outrace its cousin when fleeing predators. Following Lamarck's and Darwin's thinking, this lizard could then pass the beneficial trait of a detachable tail to its offspring. Another simple example might be a young woman who constantly tans herself on the beach. This skin tone could have a survival benefit in the form of preventing disabling sunburns and thereby allowing her to better hunt or gather and take care of her young. So far, as best as I can tell, a tanned woman has not given birth to a tanned baby.

ACCEPTANCE WITHOUT PROOF

Despite the fact that Lamarckian theories have been discredited by all of the Natural Sciences, Darwinian theories have steadily gained acceptance. Many of the more adamant proponents have not read Darwin's works. Few care to. They just believe it, like one might believe Holy Writ. It's clearly a faith issue, however. In an effort to bring light to the theory of evolution, modern science has brought many shades of darkness.

Darwin's books are historically fascinating, but they are also filled with errors. In one, Darwin proposed that South American Indians had short legs to better fit into their short canoes which they used to hunt and fish ("to survive"). One might speculate if trees ever came to be at a premium and canoes had to be made even smaller, then legs would naturally shorten as well.

Darwin often spoke of inferior races and the inferior sex. Indeed, he was very politically incorrect for our times. The full title of his most famous book, *On the Origins of Species, or Preservation of Favored Races in the Struggle for Life,* is rarely acknowledged. Many dislikable leaders, including Hitler, Stalin, and Marx, have favored his works, as did many well-known American figures in the 1930s and 1940s who promoted eugenics, the policy to weed out "inferior" people so as to create a superior, fitter race. They felt this was a form of natural selection and survival of the fittest. Fortunately, much of that quieted down as the ugliness of Nazism got louder. It has not disappeared, however.

Darwinists will sometimes point to mutations as another explanation for a species to change. This is another unfounded belief system. They ignore the scientific facts that these alterations are excedingly rare and are either damaging or insignificant. One science writer compared the effect of mutations to that of a shotgun fired at a book. They only make the book harder to read. In contrast, the sharpshooter type of mutation, only picking off a letter or two, will usually go unnoticed and disappear.

Darwin was obviously perplexed by the lack of tangible support for his theory of evolution when he asked, "Why then is not every geological formation and every stratum full of such intermediate links? Geology assuredly does not reveal any such finely graduated organic chain." The same lack of support holds true even more today. Despite an enormous number of new paleontology findings (in the hundreds of thousands), better scientific tools, and sophisticated analyses, transitional forms remain elusive. Nonetheless, one is asked to believe they will be found in the future, a notion clearly dependent on a belief system.

Darwin didn't know anything about cellular physiology, such as how a heart cell works or the functions of the DNA helix inside a fertilized ovum. Cellular biology was in its infancy and, so the story goes, he kept Gregor Mendel's book on heredity in his library but never opened it. Darwin simply likened the whole evolutionary process to processes he viewed in the neighborhood, such as breeding better carrier pigeons and raising more productive dairy cows. If they

Has Modern Science Shot Itself in the Foot?

Epigenetics (meaning "in addition to genes") is a new biological science that studies factors besides DNA that can affect gene expression.

Picture an invisible chemical blanket wrapped around each DNA helix (which contains our genes). Contained within this "blanket" are proteins that act as on/off switches for genes within the DNA itself. These proteins can be slightly altered under very specific conditions, such as changes in the mother's diet. Once a switch has been "flipped," in some cases this characteristic can be passed on to future generations.

For instance, this new science has shown that fat, yellow-furred mice that are prone to diabetes can be manipulated into having thin, mousy-brown offspring that are not prone to diabetes. And these characteristics will be handed down to subsequent generations.

So Lamarck may have been right, but only very slightly...and for entirely wrong reasons. Moreover, these newest findings don't help the theory of evolution; they in fact confound it by adding millions more missing links—links needed to explain the origin of these protein on/off switches.

could be bred into something better, surely Nature did the same. Musing in an armchair was often the scientific method of the day. Darwin particularly praised Lamarck in the third edition of *The Origin of Species*. The men thought a lot alike.

WARMED-OVER LAMARCKIANISM

The entire theory of evolution can be viewed as a Lamarckian march carried through time. If it's a favorable trait, it will be added to the gene pool. If it's not, it will be left behind. If reptiles needed to fly and there was a favorable trait to be had, it automatically became part of their gene pool. If a flat plant needed to grow vertically to compete for sunlight, it could. This is wishful thinking—a remarkable, Lamarckable fable.

Darwin was mistaken when he wrote that animals will change their inherited traits during hard times. There may have been some examples to make it seem that way, but for the most part, animals will downsize by having smaller litters, travel elsewhere for better pastures, hibernate, estivate, or eat less likable foods. Female marathon runners will often cease having menstrual periods because the body views this condition as a famine. A woman doesn't change her genetic makeup from a nonrunner who menstruates to a runner who doesn't. When a climate becomes adverse or populations are too dense, many plants will also downsize by producing fewer seeds, by slowing growth, or by going into dormancy. The key mistaken words are "changing inherited traits," not inherited *options*.

Modern medicine is facing enormous challenges from a rapid increase in antibiotic-resistant microrganisms that can cause life-threatening illnesses. This survival ability to mutate upon demand and then pass the trait to future generations is often cited as an example of natural selection. Some writers go as far as saying it actually proves the theory of evolution. Perhaps, but several important questions remain. Is the ability to change already present and then, given dire straits, comes forth? Is there a fortuitous addition of a virus that carries the resistance to the genome? We do have some very tough microbes around. Does the fact that most bacteria can go from a single microbe to more than 10 million clones in 24 hours play a role? Might not any species come up with one or two minute changes if they reproduced that many times? Supposedly, man has only been around for 150,000 years. If change comes by the ten millionth generation (like bacteria), we have a long while to wait.

Darwin was also wrong about predators and how they hunt. With rare exceptions like man, predators never overexploit populations. Other than cats, animals rarely kill for what seems to be fun. Most predators trim excesses or take out the ill, the aged, or the slowest. These are universal, natural processes. However, man has beaten the dodo bird into extinction because it was edible and friendly, destroyed the buffalo herds for sport, killed overwhelming masses of sea life with careless pollution and uncontrolled fishing, and may be destroying himself with the greenhouse effect.

Darwin's followers have allowed themselves huge Lamarckian jumps of faith, yet they tell us to believe that these gap-riddled transitions are facts. If a species wants a trait and it needs it to survive, it can make it happen, no matter how complex it might be, no matter how the genes must change, and no matter how drastically many genes may be involved.

Present evolutionary theory uses the magician's trick of throwing a brightly colored drape over a glass-paneled box with a chimplike character inside. Moments later (150,000 years), the drape is pulled away revealing a beautiful woman. Has the monkey quickly evolved or has the woman merely taken the chimp's place? Likewise, evolution may be an illusion.

■ ■ ■ ■ ■

One definition of religion listed in the *World Book* is "anything done or followed with reverence or devotion." The American Heritage Dictionary includes the phrase "an objective pursued with zeal or conscientious devotion." The *Encyclopedia Britannica* discussion of religion begins with "religion, man's relation to that which he regards as holy. The 'holy' need not be thought of as supernatural." The theory of evolution also depends on zeal and conscientious devotion, as it is yet to be proven.

Challenging Einstein's theory of relativity will hardly incite public emotions or lawsuits. No one will picket a speaker who is arguing pro or con on the theory of plate tectonics. No movie producer will select a courtroom drama to debate Newton's laws. Much more is at stake with the theory of evolution, including academic careers, personal agendas, professional agendas, individual rights, religious beliefs, past behaviors, one's livelihood, different cultures, school curriculums, public images, and church-versus-state issues.

Darwinists often say Intelligent Design is disguised religion, yet their "Creation," which is an unbelievable random big bang followed by the accidental formation of trillions of planets, requires limitless trust and belief. Not one human being can prove how we all began, but some authors of scientific books commonly say they know what happened in the first seven seconds after that explosion. Perhaps someone can go back eight seconds and tell us what preceded the explosion, what caused the explosion, and how big the stick of dynamite was.

Until Darwin's ideas are fully proven, and so far none are, they remain a faith issue. Having state-supported clerical leaders, security forces, and worship centers, Darwinism is clearly a religion in disguise.

30. SCIENCE'S REMAINING RESPONSIBILITY

"In modern science, man has crawled another step in his understanding of God. Rather than denying God, I believe science corroborates the Magnitude and Wonder of God."

—ANNABEL KITZHABER, ABOUT 1970, IN A LETTER TO HER SON DR. JOHN KITZHABER, GOVERNOR OF THE STATE OF OREGON FROM 1995 TO 2003

The beginning of life was more than a simple lightning strike on a primordial sea. The tiniest organisms require millions of moving parts. Old and new alike, they are miniature biological machines that need to find nourishment (fuel), utilize oxygen or carbon dioxide, regenerate, retain water, eliminate wastes, protect themselves from the elements, and reproduce. To have all of these mandatory processes (and many others) for life arrive by accident and simultaneously, is not believable.

And this is the easiest part of evolution to explain.

For a salmon to find a simple morsel of food, it must have the sensation of hunger, know how to locate the proper food, be ready for alternative options, be on guard for predators, know how to capture the food (and not be captured), have the external mechanisms (fins, tails, eyes) to get there and back, and have the internal mechanisms to digest the food, utilize the metabolic products, and dispose of the waste. Each step requires a moving interaction of millions of cells, processes, and chemicals. Each process, if it truly arose from evolution, should have had multiple, previous steps (links) of development. Yet, 99.9 percent of these steps remain unaccounted for.

And this is just one of many coincidences within the same species.

IMPROBABLE STORIES

Billions of difficult changes were needed to transition from a primitive pre-fish, such as the lamprey, into the modern sleek and shiny fish we all recognize. An enormous number of internal and external changes had to have occurred. This leads to many questions, such as how did all of those scales show up one at a time? Were they originally soft and useless? How were the color and shape selected? Did gills explode on the scene or arrive in useless pieces and parts over many millennia? How did an early fishlike creature give birth before there were eggs to lay? How did their genes plan ahead? The odds of any of these changes happening together are astronomical.

Taking these same thoughts a huge step further, the number of links needed to happen simultaneously for a fish to survive on land is closer to infinite. If evolution was truly responsible for the transition of life from the sea onto land, the changes would have been incredibly slow and cluttered with nonfunctional or severely impaired species. Eventually this progression would need to produce a functional set of lungs (breathing air rather than water while on the beach is a very big deal), appropriate changes in the great blood vessels (carrying larger concentrations of oxygen is another big deal), a diaphragm with flexible ribs to help the lungs expand and retract plus the appropriate muscles, a nose or some tubular apparatus to conduct air to and from the lungs (and eliminate gills), new blood chemistry to deal with increased oxygen demands (and eliminate old chemistries), a means to keep from drying out, eyelids that actually close, a new way to hear, adjustable pupils to handle bright sunlight, new night vision, natural eye lubricant, foot protection for hot sands, ways to avoid overheating during the day, a means to limit chilling at night, new ways to mate and raise offspring, an altered immune system (new diseases?), a change in sleep patterns, skills to find and digest new food, and knowledge to avoid becoming another animal's dinner. Imagine what a species might look like with different bits of different systems at different stages. They could not exist.

Although monkeys are no longer considered our direct ancestors, many biologists think they remain distant cousins. Somewhere way back among our distant grandparents all primates are said to be descendants of an ancient shrewlike animal. Monkeys showed up around 3 million years ago; we came along about 150,000 years ago. For unclear reasons, despite plenty of time, monkeys have not progressed at all, while we have moved on substantially. Primates have continued eating ticks captured on their partner's back while we have progressed to composing music, harnessing electricity, curing diseases, and flying to the moon.

During that transition period between our primate ancestors and human beings, the missing links include bipeds with weaker, shorter arms and longer legs, increased fat layers in their skin, a different immune system, partial hymens, silent ovulation, more frequent mating, much less hair, more opposing fingers, pronating forearms, and millions more sweat glands. Every monkey knows when it's time to mate; most people have no clue once Saturday night has passed.

No scientist has ever created a living entity from mere chemicals. No naturalist has ever seen a species change into an entirely new species. No biologist has caused a fish to become an amphibian or given a lizard a set of feathered wings. No geneticist can explain how a primate could have changed in so many ways to become human. The latter is much more than the mere act of standing upright, going bald, adding fat to our skin, or gaining the gift of gab. It involves unimaginably enormous changes in the genes.

Evolutionists offhandedly mention a 2-to-5 percent genetic difference between us and apes as if it were a trivial amount. One only needs to do simple math (2 percent times six billion bases) to discover that the difference is a few million chemical compounds within each cell. That's like saying Chicago and New York are nearly the same except for two million people. This 2 percent figure ignores different twists, kinks, double-backs, and electrical charges on millions of convoluted compounds.

UNSUPPORTED "TRUTH"

Despite its numerous shortcomings, the theory of evolution continues to be called a "fact," and according to some scientists, it no longer needs validation. Some support their "fact" with a fervent vigor, yet paradoxically, they quietly admit there is a growing number of missing links. They have also ignored the fact that the theory fails the tenets of the scientific method.

For evolution to have been successful, nearly every step, link, or phase, no matter how minute, starting with the primordial sea and ending with human beings, had to have happened in the right ways, at the right times, and in the right places. Had these changes happened by trial and error or by random mutations, we would be up to our elbows in fossilized mistakes.

And we are not.

The theory of evolution has yet to be supported by scientific experimentation. Efforts in the lab to recreate life have resulted only in failures, messes, and aberrations. Insects with legs growing where antennae belong are not new species. Bacteria with implanted genes are not naturally derived. Fossils of changing size or increasing complexity are only circumstantial evidence and are much more inconsistent than most people realize. The Cambrian period fossils are found thousands of feet higher than younger fossils in the Grand Canyon. Fossilized dinosaur bones are found on the surface in the Dakotas, while their possible predecessors are at the bottom of the sea. Sometimes fossils are found in the "right" order; sometimes they are not. Sometimes a logical transition actually skips to an entirely different continent, yet that part is left out of the textbook.

The argument against evolution goes far beyond Dr. Michael Behe's terrific example of a mousetrap that won't work without all of its parts in the right place. Dr. Behe calls this phenomenon *irreducible complexity*, meaning if any single part were removed from the system (reducing it), the contraption would not work. The human being has millions of these "mousetraps" in the form of intricate anatomy, chemical processes, and cellular interactions. One cannot take random chunks out of hormones and expect them to work or transplant brain cells to the feet and expect them to fight foot odor.

Is life the consequence of three-and-a-half billion years of evolution, the result of Intelligent Design, or some combination thereof? The answer is neither simple nor agreed upon. I suspect it may never be agreed upon. There have been innumerable books, articles, theses, and campus lectures supporting evolution, yet nearly everyone involved has been oblivious to the evolutionary gaps. Design, however, is readily apparent everywhere. Just look at yourself in a mirror, use your hands to write a letter, kiss a loved one, watch puppies play, or listen to birds singing.

Truth, like beauty, may be in the eyes of the beholder. Scientists will never be able to peek into the Pre-Cambrian sea and observe thousands of living species evolving into newer and different species or measure the temperature of a brontosaurus. Yet some experts claim to know "the truth" anyway. Although the theory of evolution is inadequately tested and quite different than most accepted theories, it lingers, protected under the umbrella of science.

■■■■■

If the scientific predictions are correct—that there will eventually be 100 million living species discovered and categorized on Earth—there will easily be several billion missing links realized. These calculations are compounded by the fact that many changes within any species and going between species had to have happened simultaneously. There should be millions upon millions of mistakes in the fossil records. So far, that part of the textbook is blank.

One must ask, how could there have ever been life on Earth without the coincidental combinations of correct gases to breathe, water in a liquid and usable form, atmospheric protection from the sun's damaging rays, the right distance from the sun and moon, a means to retain the sun's warmth, the presence of light, and the benefit of mostly favorable climates? How could there have been spontaneously appearing microorganisms without any intermediate preceding steps? A mix of sugar, oxygen, carbon, proteins, and water (life's key ingredients) remains a mix of the same five ingredients whether it is boiled, frozen, or microwaved. How did the ingredients come to life? How could primitive organisms have survived without the coincidental presence of mechanisms to find food, protect themselves, change locations, and reproduce? One cannot have an organism that knows how to hunt but cannot swallow, or one that can eat all it wants but has no way to produce future generations.

How does a tarantula know how to molt when it has never seen the process before? How does an octopus know how to hunt if it was orphaned at birth? How could fish evolve without the right environment, the entire correct anatomy to swim and breathe, and the coincidental recollection of where to spawn? How could there be birds if there are no worms or seeds to be had, no tree limbs for nesting, no stepwise development of wings and tail feathers to fly? How could hundreds of thousands of different insect species have come about in one or two evolutionary steps each when each species is so varied? How could tens of thousands of complex plants evolve in successive stages without the original ability to make food through photosynthesis, utilize their roots to collect water, pair up with underground fungi for nitrogen fixation, and make pollen to pass their genes to another generation?

Survival of the fittest, hibernation, echolocation, bioluminescence, reproduction, adaptations, migrations, genetic variations, all chemical laws, all physical laws, and all biological laws, usually called science, can be consequences of Intelligent Design. There are no contradictions in this assertion. No matter what we believe—and so far it's still belief systems about our origin—we continue to have a responsibility to learn every how, why, when, what, and where about life.

AFTERTHOUGHT

"Look at the animals and they will teach you;
Look at the birds and they will tell you;
Or speak to the earth and it will teach you;
Go to the fish of the sea and they will tell you
what you need to know."

—THE BOOK OF JOB

What is the value of having the presence of billions of cells in the brain and trillions more in the rest of our body without the ability to think and feel, to speak and be spoken to, and to love and be loved? Every aspect of our inner self is managed by billions of DNA compounds and several layers of hundreds of millions of proteins within each cell that somehow know how to do, when to do, and where to do their work. Most actions happen in millionths of a second, but there are some that follow very specific building plans over days, years, and even decades. If all of this (we) came about through evolution, meaning mere chance, there would have had to have been a near-infinite number of ministeps over unfathomable lengths of time. If life here truly began 3.5 billion years ago, it's not likely it would have proceeded beyond mold. And that would only be if everything went right.

■ ■ ■ ■ ■

Scientists do not know how a single ovum permits a single sperm to penetrate its exterior wall, how it sets up a chemical barrier to other sperm circling about, or how it then finds its way to the uterus. They also don't know how the monthly ovum is selected

271

out of hundreds of thousands of choices or why a certain sperm is more favored when there are hundreds of millions present. No one knows how the sperm finds its way to the egg or knows where to go once inside. Try finding a specific manila folder in a gray filing cabinet in a hundred story skyscraper. And by the way, would you have it on my desk before the day is up?

A fertilized ovum is the beginning of a person, much like the headwaters of a mighty river. It is literally the first step in a long and very complex journey that will steadily gain strength, size, momentum, and purpose. It carries the blueprint for an entirely new person, a changing and flexible how-to book that supervises everything from our conception to our last breath. Our genes control much more of our destiny than most of us realize.

As the ovum travels and implants in the uterus wall, it splits into two cells, then into four, then eight, then sixteen, and so on into the billions. In some ways, it's like a three-dimensional game of falling dominoes. Knock one down and watch several lines take off in many different yet specific directions. With each step (fall), they change color, size, shape, and function at predetermined times, until suddenly a domino becomes the first heart cell, the beginning of an artery, or the template for a bone. No scientist can truly say how a new cell knows it's time or gets the wherewithal to do its job. The final product will be a living person who can pass the same kind of instructions on to future generations.

Add up the seconds that make up nine months of a pregnancy and that will give you the barest minimum number of steps that are needed to explain our existence (hint: 24,192,000 seconds). That does not count the simultaneous steps of other animals, plants, and microorganisms, both past and present.

The scientific arguments against the theory of evolution are steadily mounting and, contrary to common perception, they do not conflict with survival of the fittest or natural selection among or within species. There are too many missing links, discovery disconnects, anatomical and functional complexities, and unexplained genetic changes, and too overwhelming a number of inexplicable and improbable coincidences, for evolution to be placed among proven scientific theories.

An enormous, rapidly growing, tidal wave of missing links is closing in on Charles Darwin's beach, yet some of the shoreline residents cannot hear the roar. Some may always be deaf.

■ ■ ■ ■ ■

Charles Darwin admitted he had no idea why a child resembled his biological parents, yet he proposed that humans descended from primates. In 1872, he famously wrote,

> If it could be demonstrated that any complex organ existed which could not possibly have been formed by numerous, successive slight modifications, my theory would ultimately break down.

This demonstration is complete.

ACKNOWLEDGMENTS

The effort needed to truly acknowledge everyone who has contributed to this work, or indeed any piece of work, would create an exhausting read and leave little space for the matters at hand. Like the bruising caused by a pea stashed beneath 20 mattresses in Hans Christian Andersen's "The Princess and the Pea," we are all impacted by unseen, minuscule events. Every thought we have ever had has some basis in another's mind; every action we take is a continuance of someone else's action or thought. One cannot study the nature of iridescent butterfly wings before the right species has been discovered. No one can guess there's a sea route taken by migrating birds unless there has been a dialogue between observers at multiple points. One cannot know that the lens of the eye has a thousand layers of transparent cells before the microscope was invented.

In a like sense, a teacher, writer, or researcher cannot be accurate if previous teachers, writers, or researchers were not accurate or honest in their works.

Although Charles Darwin borrowed from many authors—including his own grandfather, Erasmus Darwin, who wrote *Zoömonia* (1794–1796), he rarely gave credit to anyone. Try to find a bibliography. He was not the "original" thinker on the beginnings of life. Indeed, much of his work reflects prejudices, false assumptions, assumed natural laws, and feigned research projects as well as the reasonable thoughts of unnamed colleagues. Among the notables who have heartily adopted his conclusions have been Hitler, Marx, and Stalin.

Despite having a difference of opinion, I owe acknowledgment to such thoughtful writers as Stephen Jay Gould, Ernst Mayr, Carl Sagan, Lynn Margulis, E.O. Wilson, Michael Ruse, and even Richard Dawkins. These writers' observations and sometimes misinterpretations have greatly fueled my interest in the origins of life. Many of their conclusions have compelled me to respond. I owe them a debt.

A special academic thanks goes to William Paley, William Dembski, Michael Behe, Gerald L. Schroeder, Michael J. Denton, Jonathan Wells, T. Lee Baumann, Guillermo Gonzalez, Jay W. Richards, Lee Spetner, Francis Hitching, Stephen C. Meyer, John Patrick, and James Lovelock. Their works, in contrast, have helped encourage my work in many positive ways.

I remain deeply appreciative of the continued support given to me by Harvest House Publishers, their president, Bob Hawkins Jr., and their staff; and I am particularly thankful for the work done by editors Terry Glaspey and Paul Gossard. Their insightful suggestions have helped my books enormously. My most personal gratitude goes to my wife, Sherry, who has been incredibly supportive and infinitely patient. She has remained my best critic, my dearest friend, and my most trusted confidante. She also keeps me from getting into too much trouble.

Despite political pigeonholing, "open-minded" yet inflexible purveyors of tolerance, insipid intellectual constipation, nontraditional traditionalists, regressive progressives, and a landscape of hidden agendas, the billions of missing links will require billions of explanations. And their number continues to rise. Is there even time to sort them out? Or enough researchers to explain them?

I appreciate this opportunity to challenge science's royalty, the theory of evolution, with newer scientific and medical facts. There is nothing wrong with challenging any scientific theory. Where would we be if the world were still thought to be flat? To deny such questioning is to deny that Darwin theory is even science. The clothes on this emperor are missing—replaced however, by a well-Designed birthday suit.

—*Geoff Simmons, MD*
November 2006

OTHER BOOKS BY GEOFFREY SIMMONS

The Z Papers (Arbor House, Bantam)
The Adam Experiment (Arbor House, Berkley)
Pandemic (Arbor House, Berkley)
MURDOCK (Arbor House)
The Glue Factory (Beckett)
To Glue or Not To Glue (Beckett)
What Darwin Didn't Know (Harvest House)

NOTES

■■■■■

1. Copyright © 2006 Photo Researchers, Inc. All rights reserved. Used by permission.

2. Courtesy of NASA. Public domain.

3. Copyright © 2006 Photo Researchers, Inc. All rights reserved. Used by permission.

4. Copyright © 2006 Photo Researchers, Inc. All rights reserved. Used by permission.

5. Copyright © 2006 Photo Researchers, Inc. All rights reserved. Used by permission.

6. Copyright © 2006 Photo Researchers, Inc. All rights reserved. Used by permission.

7. Copyright © 2006 Photo Researchers, Inc. All rights reserved. Used by permission.

8. Copyright © 2006 Photo Researchers, Inc. All rights reserved. Used by permission.

9. Copyright © 2006 Photo Researchers, Inc. All rights reserved. Used by permission.

10. Copyright © 2006 Photo Researchers, Inc. All rights reserved. Used by permission.

BIBLIOGRAPHY

■■■■■

Agosta, William. *Bombardier Beetles and Fever Trees: A Close-up Look at Chemical Warfare and Signals in Animals and Plants.* Addison-Wesley Publishing Company, 1995.

Amato, Ivan. *Super Vision: A New View of Nature.* Harry N. Abrams, Inc., Publishers, 2003.

Baker, Nick. *The Amateur Naturalist: A New Look at a Classic Subject.* HarperCollins Publishers, Ltd., 2004.

Barker, Rodney. *And the Waters Turned to Blood.* Simon and Schuster, 1998.

Barlow, George W. *The Cichlid Fishes: Nature's Grand Design in Evolution.* Perseus Publishing, 2000.

Behe, Michael J. *Darwin's Black Box.* New York: Simon and Schuster, 1996.

Benyus, Janine M. *Biomimicry: Innovation Inspired by Nature.* Harper-Collins Publishers, 2002.

Brownless, Shannon. "Blast from the Vast." *Discover* magazine, December 2003, pp. 51-57.

Bruemmer, Fred. *Glimpses of Paradise: The Marvel of Massed Animals.* Firefly Books (U.S.), Inc., 2002.

Cahill, Mark. *One Heartbeat Away: Your Journey into Eternity.* BDM Publishing, 2005.

Cawardine, Mark. *Smithsonian Extreme Nature.* HarperCollins Publishers, 2005.

Chernoff, Barry. "In His Own Words." *Discover* magazine, July 2004, pp. 58-65.

Chinery, Michael. *Poisoners and Pretenders: Secrets of the Rain Forest.* Crabtree Publishing Company, 2000.

Coburn, Phillip S., et al. "Enterococcus faecalis senses target cells and in response expresses cytolysin." *Science* magazine, December 2004, pp. 2270-2272.

Davis, Percival, Dean A. Kenyon, and Charles B. Thaxton. *Of Pandas and People: The Central Question of Biological Origins.* Haughton Publishing Company, 1989.

Dembski, William A. *The Design Revolution: Answering the Toughest Questions About Intelligent Design.* Colorado Springs, CO: InterVarsity Press, 2004.

Dennis, Jerry. *It's Raining Frogs and Fishes: Four Seasons of Natural Phenomena and Oddities of the Sky.* HarperCollins Publishers, 1992.

Denton, Michael. *Nature's Destiny: How the Laws of Biology Reveal Purpose in the Universe.* The Free Press, 1998.

Downer, John. *Weird Nature: An Astonishing Exploration of Nature's Strangest Behavior.* Firefly Books (U.S.), 2002.

Eisner, Thomas, Maria Eisner, and Melody Siegler. *Secret Weapons: Defenses of Insects, Spiders, Scorpions and Other Many-Legged Creatures.* Belknap Press of Harvard University Press, 2005.

Elam, Kimberly. *Geometry of Design: Studies in Proportion and Composition.* Princeton Architectural Press, 2001.

Elliott, Lang. *A Guide to Wildlife Sounds.* Stackpole Books, 2005.

Fernandez-Armesto, Felipe. *Ideas That Changed The World.* DK Publishing, Inc., 2003.

Flannery, Tim, and Peter Schouten. *Astonishing Animals: Extraordinary Creatures and the Fantastic Worlds They Inhabit.* Atlantic Monthly Press, 2004.

Folger, Tim. "Tabletop Physics." *Discover* magazine, October 2005, pp. 56-57.

Fox, Karen C. "Faster Than They Should Be." *Discover* magazine, 2/06, pp. 22-23.

Freeman, Scott. *Biological Science.* Pearson Prentice Hall, 2005.

Friend, Tim. *Animal Talk: Breaking the Codes of Animal Language.* The Free Press, 2004.

Goho, A. "Quick Fix: How Invasive Seaweed Repairs Itself." *Science News,* 04/02/05, p. 214.

Gonzalez, Guillermo, and Jay W. Richards. *The Privileged Planet: How*

Our Place in the Cosmos Is Designed for Discovery. Regnery Publishing, Inc., 2004.

Gordon, David George. *The Compleat Cockroach.* Ten Speed Press, 1996.

Gross, Michael. *Life on the Edge: Amazing Creatures Thriving in Extreme Environments.* Perseus Publishing, 2001.

Halberstram, Yotta, and Judith Leventhal. *Small Miracles.* Adams Media Corporation, 1997.

Hitching, Francis. *The Neck of the Giraffe: Where Darwin Went Wrong.* Ticknor and Fields, 1982.

Kraut, J. "How do enzymes work?" *Science,* vol. 242, pp. 533-540.

Lacrampe, Corine. *Sleep and Rest in Animals.* Firefly Books, Ltd., 2003.

Lavers, Chris. *Why Elephants Have Big Ears: Understanding Patterns of Life on Earth.* St. Martin's Press, 2001.

Levy, Charles Kingsley. *Evolutionary Wars: A Three Billion-Year Arms Race.* W.H. Freeman and Company, 1999.

Lide, David R. *Handbook of Chemistry and Physics,* 86th ed. CRC Press, 2005.

Linden, Eugene. *The Octopus and the Orangutan: More True Stories of Animal Intrigue, Intelligence, and Ingenuity.* Penguin Group, 2002.

Lord, M.G. "Impossible Journey: It Will Take More than Rocket Science to Survive a Trip to Mars." *Discover* magazine, June 2006, pp. 38-45.

Lovelock, James. *Gaia: A New Look at Life on Earth.* Oxford University Press, 1987.

———. *The Ages of Gaia: A Biography of Our Living Earth.* W.W. Norton & Company, 1988.

Margulis, Lynn. *Symbiotic Planet: A New Look at Evolution.* Basic Books, 1998.

Martin, Jobe. *The Evolution of a Creationist.* Biblical Discipleship Publishers, 2002.

Milius, Susan. "Warm-Blooded Plants?" *Science News,* 12/13/03, pp. 379-381.

_____. "When to Change Sex." *Science News,* 01/17/04, pp. 40-41.

_____. "Myth of the Bad-Nose Birds." *Science News,* 8/20/05, pp. 120-123.

Moreira, N. "Sleepless in Seaworld." *Science News,* July 2, 2005.

Norell. Mark. *Unearthing the Dragon: The Great Feathered Dinosaur Discovery.* PI Press, 2005.

Paley, William. *Paley's Natural Theology.* Richardson, Lord & Holbrook, and Crocker and Brewster, 1831.

Plotkin, Mark J. *Medicine Quest: In Search of Nature's Healing Secrets.* Penguin Books, 2000.

Purser, Bruce. *Jungle Bugs: Masters of Camouflage and Mimicry.* Firefly Books (U.S.), Inc., 2003.

Schmidt-Nielsen, Knut. *Animal Physiology: Adaptation and Environment,* 5th ed. Cambridge University Press, 1997.

_____. *Scaling: Why Is Animal Size So Important?* Cambridge University Press, 1984.

Seppa, N. "Attack on Elephantiasis." *Science* magazine, June 25, 2005.

Sheer, Lynn. *Tall Blondes: A Book About Giraffes.* Andrew McMeel Publishing, 1997.

Shiga, David. "Poisonous Partnership," *Science News,* February 26, 2005.

Shuker, Dr. Karl P.N. *The Hidden Powers of Animals: Uncovering the Secrets of Nature.* Reader's Digest. 2001.

Siebert, Charles. "Unintelligent Design." *Discover* magazine, March 2006.

Spetner, Lee. *Not By Chance.* The Judaica Press, 1998.

Steele, Edward J., et al. *Lamarck's Signature: How Retrogenes Are Changing Darwin's Natural Selection Paradigm.* Perseus Books, 1998.

Stewart, Amy. *The Earth Moved: On the Remarkable Achievements of Earthworms.* Algonquin Books of Chapel Hill, 2004.

Stewart, Ian. *Life's Other Secret: The New Mathematics of the Living World.* John Wiley and Sons, Inc., 1998.

Strogatz, Steven. *Sync: The Emerging Science of Spontaneous Order.* Hyperion, 2003.

Sumner, Judith. *The Natural History of Medicinal Plants.* Timber Press, Inc., 2000.

Tyrrell, Esther Quesada. *Hummingbirds: Their Life and Behavior.* Crown Publishers, Inc., 1985.

Thomas, David N. *Frozen Oceans: The Floating World of Pack Ice.* Firefly Books (U.S.), Inc., 2004.

Travis, John. "All the World's a Phage." *Science News,* 7/12/03.

Vogel, Steven. *Cats' Paws and Catapults: Mechanical Worlds of Nature and People.* W.W. Norton and Company, 1998.

Wagner, Edward K., and Martinez J. Hewlett. *Basic Virology.* Blackwell Science, Inc., 1999.

Wakeford, Tom. *Liaisons of Life.* John Wiley and Sons, Inc. 2001.

Waldbauer, Gilbert. *What Good Are Bugs?* Harvard University Press, 2003.

Wilson, E.O. *Sociobiology: The New Synthesis.* Harvard University Press, 2000.

Winnick, Pamela R. *A Jealous God: Science's Crusade Against Religion.* Nelson Current, 2005.

Wolfe, David, W. *Tales from the Underground: A Natural History of Subterranean Life.* Perseus Publishing, 2001.

Where's the Science?

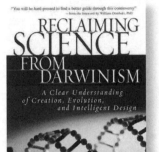

The concern that haunted Charles Darwin—and has dogged Darwinism for 150 years—is now an inescapable conclusion: *The science is not there.*

Today, we have mountains of evidence that relates to the origins of life. *Reclaiming Science from Darwinism* shows you why that evidence indisputably supports purpose and design in the cosmos…and decisively exposes Darwinism's failures. Using enlightening analogies, pointed examples, and clear explanations, Kenneth Poppe digs into these issues and more:

- mind-sets that undermine objectivity in both science and religion

- the impossibility of the first cell coming about by blind luck

- the mathematical *im*probabilities of random improvement in species

- scientists' fantasies regarding extraterrestrial life

- unsupported assumptions about bridging the gaps in the fossil record with "good" mutations

Up-to-date, straightforward, and spiced with humor as well as helpful graphics, this resource offers you solid information so you can judge for yourself where the science really is.

Excellent for students and parents, as well as educators who want to present a complete picture of origins science

What Darwin didn't know lies at the tips of your fingers... and everywhere else in your anatomy.

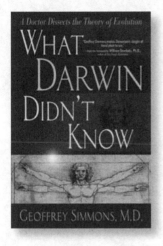

The founder of evolutionary theory didn't know that the function of every cell and every system in your body follows an intricate DNA blueprint. In fact, he didn't know much about the human body at all.

Drawing on the most recent research as well as years of clinical work, Geoffrey Simmons tells the real story about your amazing complexity:

- *The brain* resembles a continent swept by electrical hurricanes and chemical tidal waves that somehow makes sense out of reality

- *A fertilized egg* makes a journey as complex as the path of a golf ball that rolls 30 miles and lands precisely in the 18th hole of a course it's never seen

- *The immune system* contains multiple defenses that confine trillions of microorganisms to your skin, like passengers innocently sunning themselves on the deck of a cruise ship

What Darwin Didn't Know pictures the wonders of the human body in their true context—a marvelous system fashioned by an infinitely wise Designer.